D1470251

Implementing
World Class IT
Strategy

Implementing World Class IT Strategy

How IT Can Drive Organizational Innovation

Peter A. High

Foreword by Filippo Passerini

JB JOSSEY-BASS™
A Wiley Brand

Cover design by Wiley
Cover image © iStock.com/koya79

Author photo by Morad Boroomand, Image Perfect.

Copyright © 2014 by John Wiley & Sons, Inc. All rights reserved.
Published by Jossey-Bass
A Wiley Brand
One Montgomery Street, Suite 1200, San Francisco, CA 94104-4594—www.josseybass.com

Jossey-Bass books and products are available through most bookstores. To contact Jossey-Bass
directly call our Customer Care Department within the U.S. at 800-956-7739, outside the U.S.
at 317-572-3986, or fax 317-572-4002.

Wiley publishes in a variety of print and electronic formats and by print-on-demand. Some
material included with standard print versions of this book may not be included in e-books or
in print-on-demand. If this book refers to media such as a CD or DVD that is not included in
the version you purchased, you may download this material at http://booksupport.wiley.com. For
more information about Wiley products, visit www.wiley.com.

Library of Congress Cataloging-in-Publication Data is on file.

High, Peter A.
    Implementing world class IT strategy : how IT can drive organizational innovation / Peter
A. High.
        pages cm. — (The Jossey-Bass business & management series)
    Includes bibliographical references and index.
    ISBN 978-1-118-63411-0 (hardcover); ISBN 978-1-118-63408-0 (ebk.);
    ISBN 978-1-118-63417-2 (ebk.)
        1. Information technology—Management.   2. Information technology—
Technological innovations.   3. Technological innovations—Management.
4. Management information systems.   I. Title.
HD30.2.H542   2014
658.4'038—dc23
                                                                          2014022040

Printed in the United States of America
FIRST EDITION
HB Printing   10 9 8 7 6 5 4

The Jossey-Bass
Business & Management Series

Contents

For my father and mother

If opportunity doesn't knock, build a door.
—Milton Berle

Foreword

As group president of Global Business Services (GBS) and chief information officer for Procter & Gamble, I have more than a passing interest in the strategic role that CIOs—and their entire IT organizations—can and should play within their businesses.

After spending more than thirty years within the broader field of information technology, living in six countries, and overseeing the implementation of hundreds, if not thousands, of IT projects, I'm passionate about elevating the role of CIOs. When CIOs think beyond technology to deliver true relevance and value to the business, the results are powerful.

I first crossed paths with Peter High when he interviewed me for his "CIO-Plus" series that was published in his "Technovation" column in Forbes.com. In his interviews with leading CIOs, Peter explored additional responsibilities IT leaders have assumed beyond traditional IT roles, especially as they have become more business-centric in terms of their skill sets. As that conversation continued, and as we have maintained an ongoing dialogue since, I realized that he and I were kindred spirits in our belief in the power of the role of CIO.

That series, and the focus of Peter's broader work, suggests that at least some IT leaders are becoming much more strategic to the companies they serve. Peter is delivering the right message about CIOs at precisely the right time.

At P&G, fundamentally, the mission of our GBS team is about transforming the way business is done. While technology is completely different from how it was just five years ago, and even more pervasive, our basic approach within GBS has not changed: we want to create capabilities that bring relevance and value to the business.

In this book, Peter emphasizes the need for IT strategy to be woven into the broader strategy of the company, and that it not be developed in a vacuum. He notes the importance of linking the plans of the corporation and those of the business units and divisions to those of IT and ultimately connecting the dots to the project work that IT undertakes. This cascade that results ensures a line of sight from the projects that individual contributors are working on to the objectives of the company. This is exactly how we think about things at P&G and within GBS.

It may seem ironic, but even though we are IT professionals at a global consumer packaged goods company, technology is the last thing we think about when we are deciding what is needed to bring value for the business. We always start with the end in mind, and we never fall in love with technology for technology's sake. It's a very deliberate process.

We start by looking at trends in the world that are here to stay. What economic, social, and demographic issues are having an impact on the world, and what do they mean for our business? Then we look at trends in business in general and in consumer packaged goods specifically. We anticipate our own business needs and think about whether there are solutions that we could apply across various parts of our business. What IT strategies will help us stay in control and best manage the trends? Then, and only then, do we think about what technologies will fuel those strategies and deliver real business value.

Technology comes last; it's a means to an end.

This process starts with our people—all six thousand GBS team members. As part of our organizational design, our GBS team members are embedded in the business, literally placed through-out the company, co-located with our business partners. This ena-bles them to spend a lot of time *understanding* the business.

Our GBS team members are business people first and tech-nology people second. They speak the language that our business partners speak. We want to understand the business so well that we detect what is needed and understand what is possible. We are listening to the needs of the business and bringing an ear to that unmet need.

Developing a unified plan is a bit of a challenge for us because we have very diversified work, but it's critical that we have a clearly defined strategy and that our goals and vision are inclu-sive. That's one of the reasons why we have made communica-tions part of our strategic framework. We are very deliberate in the way we communicate—ensuring our communications are clear, actionable, and inspiring—and that goes a long way. Our various teams may have different executions or action items, but we are all united under the same vision.

Peter also stresses the need to refresh plans so that they do not become stagnant. This is critical. We think about strategy as an ongoing journey. The world is changing so fast that we must stay constantly agile, have flexibility, and anticipate what will be needed. We build a network of collaboration around what is possi-ble, then redirect resources and work to what is needed.

At P&G, the consumer is our boss. In GBS, we continue to be laser focused on being transformative and innovative so P&G can win with—and bring value to—consumers and sharehold-ers. Much of our focus now is on the processes and real-time data that improve our decision making and provide deeper consumer insights. Technology is more the catalyst today than ever.

One other point of Peter's strikes a chord with me: the need to include measurement in one's plans. He notes that strategic plans must have success metrics associated with them, and "that which gets measured gets done." This element is often lacking in strategies of other companies I have been exposed to. Just like the model that Peter introduces herein, we also ensure that the progress of our strategic plans can be measured.

This all starts with the CIO. We have to be able to anticipate what is needed, be in a position to know what is possible, and respond fast with solutions that will be relevant and add value. And, perhaps most important, we need to be able to set the strategy in place that ensures everyone in the organization understands and is able to carry out the mission. Peter's ideas in this book will provide you and your team with a path to success.

—Filippo Passerini
Group president of Global Business Services
and chief information officer, Procter & Gamble

Implementing World Class IT Strategy

1

"Techtonic" Plates

How quickly do major changes and new disruptions come to pass in twenty-first-century information technology? I think of these changes like the tectonic plates of geology because they can be huge and obvious, like an earthquake, but they are often subtle. Suppose as a chief information officer (CIO) you are given the task of preparing the company for an event that will occur four years in the future. This may be difficult to imagine for most executives who have major deliverables on a week-to-week or month-to-month basis, but that's what this book is about—the fact that massive shifts are taking place in your business IT landscape very quickly that have short- and long-term consequences for your company's bottom line and the strategies that make or break it. More often than not, these changes are subtle, but it is important to pick up on this subtlety and to determine how these changes might have an impact on your company either as an opportunity or as a threat. Either you will recognize them, or perhaps a competitor will before you do, and seize an advantage.

Large companies, especially publicly traded ones and yours perhaps as well, are understandably sensitive to *quarterly* reporting, as they must share progress or lack thereof quarter-by-quarter with analysts and shareholders. Quarterly plans are almost by definition more tactical than strategic. Unfortunately, many companies myopically use these as their primary planning function. Others extend them to an annual plan without ample consideration for the time period beyond the year ahead, which is still myopic and does not lend itself well to creative, innovative thinking—especially for

IT departments whose technology has become so central to corporate activity today that they can only be truly successful if they can be both nimble and aware of the future. A further-looking, visionary strategic mind-set is the hallmark of World Class IT.

For a moment let's grant ourselves the luxury of an event for which we have four ("long") years to prepare. Let's put ourselves in the shoes of Gerry Pennell, CIO of the London 2012 Summer Olympics. What can we learn from his challenge and response about what CIOs need to be thinking? We'll follow his case through much of this chapter.

IT's Gold Medal

In November of 2008, Gerry Pennell became CIO for the ultimate world sporting and cultural event, the Olympic Games, whose cauldron would be lit by the Olympic torch in London on July 27, 2012, and burn for a fortnight. The Beijing Olympics had recently concluded, and he stared down the road at nearly four years of planning and execution as part of the event's top organizing committee. The scale of what he had to pull off coupled with the high bar set by the example of Beijing were motivation enough for Pennell to assemble a team, and to begin to set a plan. But his early steps were complicated by the fact that the strategic plans for the other functions the committee oversaw were in their nascent stages at best. To Pennell, that meant setting a direction for the technological approach to the Games that would still be malleable enough to change as he engaged further with his fellow committee leaders. He couldn't wait for them to get started.

Pennell's decision to forge ahead in planning without complete guidance from his peers stands in contrast to how a lot of CIOs act in the absence of concrete plans from the corporation of which they are a part. Too many of them match inaction with inaction, rather than proceeding with IT's own vision of where the company will be several years out and information technology's role in realizing that vision. Given the long-term nature of so many

IT investments, often with multiyear depreciation or amortization schedules, it behooves IT to take the initiative in pushing the rest of the organization to develop clear, well-articulated plans, and, in the absence of those, to set the example for the rest of the corporation by doing so itself.

In Pennell's case, the four-year time horizon forced him to think more than the average CIO not just about strategic flexibility but also about shifts in the "techtonic" plates in a four-year period. In any given quarter, business-changing innovations may not be readily apparent. An IT leader must possess skills and perhaps staff related to research and development, so that he or she remains abreast of these innovations in order to evaluate the potential value that using them would bring the company. This means, for example, not only noticing a new product launch from a well-known company but also not letting creative new products or services launched by small, less well-known companies pass under the radar. Reflecting back on the time period between the 2008 and 2012 Summer Olympics, it is interesting to think of the number of now-pervasive technologies that either were in their infancy or did not exist in that interval:

- In 2008 the iPhone, which brought apps to the forefront for consumers and later for companies, was only a year old, and Apple had sold less than ten million phones worldwide. By contrast, in each of the first two quarters of 2012, more than thirty million iPhones sold worldwide.[1]
- Twitter gained prominence at the South by Southwest conference in 2007, but it was not the force to be reckoned with that it would be in 2012.
- Facebook surpassed MySpace in traffic only in April of 2008.
- Although the term *cloud computing* already had been coined, the concept was still in the early stages of development and practice.
- The first iPad would not be introduced until April of 2010.

It is worth mentioning that most aspects of social media were not officially permitted at the 2008 games or in China in general, and as of this writing, one still cannot use Facebook or Twitter in that country. Therefore, Pennell could not translate the technology blueprint from Beijing to London any more than he could translate its Mandarin to English.

Many IT executives assume that previously developed IT plans are more sustainable than they really are. The problem is the quick emergence of soon-to-be-indispensable technologies. Depending on plans whose assumptions are no longer valid, largely operating on assumptions made in the past, is bad business, clearly. IT executives need to be serious about their research and development role, asking themselves questions such as

- What technologies have just emerged that neither you nor your competitors have thought much about that will become critical technologies tomorrow or next year?
- Do you have someone on your team investigating them?
- Is there a part of your IT strategy that makes space for such investigation?
- Do you have ties to the venture capital community, the start-up community, or both, so that you can develop shortcuts to these insights?
- Do any of the insights spark thoughts on new innovations that might be undertaken?
- Is your operation running well enough that you can afford to carve off sufficient time to undertake this work?

Pennell was actually brought on board the 2012 Olympic Organizing Committee before many of his colleagues, so IT had one of the longest lead times and Pennell put that crucial time to use. In its early days he developed a scope, a budget, and a full IT strategy, planting a stake in the ground, so to speak. He also made sure not to drive it in so deeply that he couldn't move it later on. Facing four uncertain years, he had to keep it adjustable. To this end, he and his team noted hypotheses and assumptions embedded in the plans; thus, when the inevitable need for change occurred, agreement with his colleagues could be forged more easily, the new plans could be ratified, and execution could begin as soon as possible.

Pennell was deliberate about not seeking perfection in an early IT plan because, as he explained it, "The fixed time horizon drives IT leaders to be satisfied with proceeding after testing plans to 80% confidence. IT leaders have a tendency to want to get to 100%, but one gives up speed in the process."[2] Perfect is unattainable, so seeking it out is a fool's errand, whereas developing a practical and implementable plan that the rest of the organization can get behind is a recipe for success. One should think of developing agile plans that can be tested, and as reality suggests that certain aspects of the plans are no longer valid, develop a new objective to pursue. This requires constant iteration with one's colleagues outside of IT. Hired ahead of many of his peers, and given how much was at stake once the Games began, Pennell had little choice but to adhere to such an approach.

The forced choice was a blessing. In most industries, the pace of change is not quite as fast and the stakes for any single two-week period not as significant as the two crowning weeks of the industry known as the Olympic Games. As a result, in many companies and industries, too often plans are constructed and then not revisited. As a result, they become stale and do not reflect reality. What is worse, they suggest that the CIO is not sufficiently engaging his or her peers and colleagues to identify when change is necessary.

Pennell had to continue to modify his plans right up until the final days (and in some cases hours) before the moment on July 27 when 204 petals of flame reached the cauldron of the 2012 London games. For example, on July 22, Bradley Wiggins became the first

British cyclist to win the Tour de France. Though cycling was to be a focal sport, there would be increased emphasis and pressure from the media on the initial road cycling events, leading to some operational challenges in technology.

It should also be noted that Pennell was not foolish enough to think he could accomplish all of this alone, or even that his team could do so without the aid of partners with deep expertise in the many areas that are essential to an Olympics. This meant developing solid processes for vendor segmentation, procurement, and management. It also meant that his team needed to have depth of expertise in project management, vendor management, and change management.

To my great pleasure (and probably to yours as well), Pennell's efforts did not go unnoticed. For his trouble, he was named an Officer of the Order of the British Empire, conferred upon him as part of the 2013 New Year Honours at Buckingham Palace. This might make more traditional awards bestowed upon CIOs seem a little less impressive, but it also demonstrates how extraordinary a job a CIO can do.

Gerry Pennell's accomplishments are at the heart of what this book hopes to facilitate for executives everywhere: developing IT strategies that anticipate and change in response to disruptions and that translate down to great implementation. This book is also about something more. It's about how IT can become a tremendous force for improving the strategic work of the company as a whole, as well as the company's other divisions, in ways that directly add to the net value of all.

If the Olympics seems like an inaccessible example to you, what about an example from the U.S. Federal Government?

Strategy, IT, and Public or Private Sectors

Some would guess that there is less of a need to create meaningful strategic plans in the public sector than in the private sector.

After all, the public sector does not exhibit the pressures of competition and the profit motive that the private sector does. When Vivek Kundra was appointed the first-ever U.S. Federal CIO on March 5, 2009, at a mere thirty-four years old, he had already been a government IT executive at the county, city, and state levels. He understood that when an executive first comes into office, people anticipate change and there is political capital to spend. That said, the window for enacting change does not stay open long; soon people revert naturally to old ways of doing things, especially in the government. As time goes on, cynics may even actively work against the change.

So just as Pennell felt the need to forge ahead without waiting on others, Kundra too had an acute sense of the need to step out in front with strategy and related ideas.

Developing a Federal IT Strategy

As Kundra put it, "You need to think about the results you want to achieve, and then develop the plan to get there. You also want to simplify things wherever possible. We did so by limiting ourselves to five areas of focus."[3]

Those five areas were

- Ensuring openness and transparency
- Lowering the cost of government
- Focusing on cyber-security
- Developing participatory democracy
- Improving the capacity to innovate[4]

These focus areas are not expressions of mere technological capabilities. They are broad, strategic goals grounded in public priorities and values. This is exactly the sort of visionary, strategic thinking exemplified by other outstanding IT thinkers on behalf of their organizations. By declaring these five objectives, Kundra could more effectively provide direction to his team, to the government complex more generally, and to the public. When new ideas were proposed, they were to align with one or more of these objectives.

Driving the Strategy Forward with Fresh Ideas

Rather than simply wait for the ideas to flow, however, Kundra had a number of them himself. For one, in May of 2009, two months after his appointment, Kundra announced the Data.gov platform, which was intended to provide public access to the raw data of the executive branch in order to foster public participation and private sector innovation. The idea stemmed from an initiative that he had undertaken in his prior role as chief technology officer of Washington, D.C. The site sought to become "a repository for all the information the government collects," excluding data that is private and restricted for national security reasons.[5]

The next month, Kundra implemented what was called the Federal IT Dashboard, the purpose of which was to track nearly $80 billion in IT spending, identifying waste and generating considerable savings. Agency and department CIOs' pictures and names were listed next to each of the projects they undertook. As Kundra explained, "This was a level of transparency that had never been in place before, and a wonderful thing happened: people started to cancel projects within their IT portfolios, saving the taxpayer money in the process."[6] The fact that they did so proactively was all the better.

Having pulled off a number of successes in his first year on the job, Kundra developed new layers to his five-focus-area strategy. At a time when government agencies were not yet buying into cloud computing, Kundra understood the transformative nature of this model. At the end of 2010, he was given two months to develop a strategy on federal adoption of cloud computing as a means of controlling costs. Within that time, he published the

Federal Cloud Computing Strategy.[7] Thus began a "cloud-first" policy across the government, which now serves as a model for government IT organizations around the world seeking to increase efficiencies with fewer resources.

Related to this strategy, Kundra developed Apps.gov, enabling government agencies to use cloud services related to major areas such as business intelligence, CRM, and collaboration.

Kundra's plans were strikingly ambitious. He was not looking to make incremental change. In a powerful, newly created role at the commencement of a new administration, change was expected of him, and he delivered by linking the changes he sought to strategic objectives, which themselves were linked to the value he and the administration wanted to achieve. In the course of his work he laid out and followed the steps that CIOs (and *all* executives) should aspire to follow and that this book will reflect:

- He developed a vision and a strategy based on identified value and communicating it using simple, easy-to-understand terminology.

- He provided success metrics and milestones that he and others could track to gauge progress along the way (transparency was a key tenet).

- He identified the levers that could be pulled, and then developed projects that would help pull them.

- He documented touchpoints with the various agencies and departments where applicable, recognizing that he needed to "market" this plan and influence others in order to accomplish it. Although he had power in his new role, it was not absolute.

When Kundra was named *Information Week*'s Chief of the Year for 2009, then U.S. chief performance officer Jeffrey Zients noted in the profile of Kundra, "Across 20 years in the private sector, I've worked with dozens of CIOs. Some are strong operators, and others are good strategists. Often times those two things are not correlated, and they're often inversely correlated. Vivek is in a league of his own, because he's both."[8]

The CIO: From Process-Centric to Strategic

The role of CIO has changed markedly. For a long time, the primary value of CIOs lay in directing the automation of processes. In so doing, CIOs would help the businesses that they served remove human error and save time and money in the process. After that, a second wave of CIOs engaged the rest of the company to develop process improvements. IT became a hub of experts in disciplines such as Lean, Six Sigma, kaizen, and others like these. IT added tremendous value by bringing process reengineering discipline to the company, making company operations more efficient. Of course, process-centric IT leadership continues, largely reacting to what is already in the organization and making it better rather than thinking about a new vision for what the company may soon need to become. CIOs who successfully led these initiatives harvested the low-hanging fruit. These were more tactical than strategic activities, on balance. There are changes afoot, however, as the examples of Pennell and Kundra should suggest. Still, even today many CIOs are not invited to be a part of the conversation when future vision is discussed.

Some of the best insights into the ever-changing role of the CIO come from people who lead companies that serve the CIO. Here are two.

The Need to Get Intimate

As president and CEO of Red Hat, the $1.5 billion global provider of community-powered open source software solutions, Jim Whitehurst has a reason to speak with CIOs on a regular basis, and has seen the evolution of the role as IT has become more core to a wider array of businesses. He says,

> Most of the major business trends today have meaningful IT components to them, no matter the industry. As a result, IT needs to be much more woven into the planning process of the rest of the organization, or it will be left behind. In the past, it was appropriate for IT to pursue version 1.0 of a project, and then six months later to pursue version 2.0. Now that information is becoming more strategic, and IT is involved in so much more, the pace of change is that much greater. When business is moving faster than the pace of the IT department's release cycles, IT needs to change. It requires that IT become much more agile, collaborative, and that it embrace service-oriented architecture.[9]

This requires that the CIO and his or her team achieve a level of intimacy with the rest of the organization far beyond what has been typical. IT leaders need to be involved in the strategy-setting meetings so that they hear when strategic priorities are changing. They need to have more business savvy to anticipate how changes in the competitive landscape or the marketplace could affect the strategic plans and therefore the IT priorities of the company.

Formal strategic planning is critical, but plans will change, and IT must be able to change its own plans quickly and assist the broader company to do so, on the basis of changes in reality. A plan is necessary but needs to be flexible. As World War I German field marshal Helmuth von Moltke the Elder said, "No plan survives contact with the enemy."

Value: The Ticket to Ride

As the CEO of NetApp, a business-to-business enterprise, Tom Georgens has seen a growing number of CIOs who have come to realize that the path toward increased relevance and inclusion of the CIO is for that person to demonstrate value on a par with other C-level executives. He says, "CIOs who wish to gain access to the CEO's strategy-setting sessions and remain as a full-fledged member of that forum need to demonstrate how IT will create competitive advantage on a par with others who are at the table."[10]

Fortunately, the means of doing so are better today than ever before. Georgens says, "Enabling the company to make better decisions and serve customers better is a competitive advantage CIOs can deliver."

The invitation for a CIO to attend strategy-setting meetings with the rest of the executives of the company is not guaranteed; a first-time invitation does not mean that future invitations will come. The CIO must strive to communicate the enhanced value delivered through IT again and again, and engage the rest of IT leadership in so doing as well.

Georgens acknowledges that when he says, "Many CIOs take on their role with a mandate to cut costs. CIOs tend to be quite good at that. If they are not careful, however, they will be associated only with that single lever of value." CIOs must push to be recognized as top-line contributors. The only way to do so effectively is to be more cognizant of how the company creates value, by garnering insights directly from customers (current and potential) whenever possible and devising solutions that will help the organization get to value more quickly. It begins with the CIO weaving him- or herself and the rest of the IT leadership team into the strategy of the company to a greater extent.

Greg Carmichael also sounds this note. Now president and COO of Fifth Third Bancorp, he was formerly the CIO of that company and of Emerson Electric Company before it. He rose to his current position from an IT role due to his ability to think about value to the business in a way not typical of CIOs. He says,

"Too many CIOs get mired in day-to-day firefighting." He adds, "First, a CIO must think about simplification of technology to create space for his or her team to think about value creation. There is no value creation in firefighting." Carmichael goes on to point out hierarchies of value that can be achieved:

> To be truly strategic, CIOs need to think about how value is created. Many are good at cost cutting, but this is almost by definition a backward looking exercise— optimizing something that is already in place. This is not strategic. CIOs need to think about what future possibilities there are to leverage technology for new value and top-line growth. This is what differentiates the strategic CIO.[11]

The Trends Are Good

Having worked with a great number of leading chief information officers across a wide array of industries and geographies, I am impressed by how much progress this community has made. The average CIO is shifting from reactive to proactive, from day-to-day operator to forward-looking innovator, from junior member of the C-suite of executives to a rightful peer to the rest of the executive team. As I have written elsewhere, two trends highlight these facts. First, CIOs are increasingly asked to take on responsibilities in addition to their IT duties, such as heading up HR, procurement, supply chain, innovation, shared services organizations, and more.[12] I have referred to this trend as the "CIO-plus." The other trend is exemplified by Greg Carmichael—the CIO who goes on to become CEO or COO.[13] The number one trait of executives who have made this rise is an ability to think about business strategy and business value first and technology implications second. This is still not the common way of thinking among IT executives, but the community of CIOs is making great progress.

Truly Strategic IT

Ensuring that IT aligns its activities to value-driven strategic imperatives requires it to have means of formulating, reviewing, and updating strategic plans. As I hope you will find through the examples of many great IT leaders throughout this book, as well as through the methodology described herein, there is a better way to do this, and the rewards for the CIO and for the companies that do so are abundant.

In the coming chapters, I will introduce a strategic framework that will help the IT leader not only formulate his or her own plans (the topic of Chapter Five) but also work with the heads of other divisions of the companies to better formulate theirs. This latter point may seem strange. Shouldn't the divisional leaders be responsible for their own plans without the need for the IT leader to get involved during the course of their formulation? Chapter Two provides an overview of why the CIO must get more involved, as both an offensive and a defensive measure.

Chapter Three provides an overview of how best to create IT mission statements. Missions are not used by all companies, to say nothing of all IT departments, but they help clarify the value that IT proposes to contribute to the company and the customers of the company. Especially in the absence of strong plans from the rest of the organization, an IT mission statement is like a flag planted in the ground for the rest of the organization to see and to comment on if necessary.

Chapter Four provides steps for the CIO to take in order to help the company and its divisions better articulate strategic plans. A variety of CIOs have done this so well that they have taken over the strategic planning process of the entire company. These CIOs lead the IT organizations of companies as diverse as $1 billion Red Robin Gourmet Burgers to the $2.5 billion chemicals company Olin Corporation to $6.3 billion Great Atlantic & Pacific Tea Company (better known as A&P) to $45 billion agriculture behemoth CHS, Inc. In addition, in 2013, the CIO of $15 billion Qantas Airways Limited became the chief strategy officer of the company. Note that none of these are explicitly IT companies the way Google or Intel are, and yet the value derived from having the IT leader responsible for strategy has been profound in each case.

Chapter Five provides an overview of how best for the CIO to sift through the plans of each of the other parts of the organization, determine how best to contribute to each, but then determine what IT-specific plans must be created as a result of that. For example, if there are mobility themes to multiple strategic plans of the company, IT must create its own plan to put together the right people, processes, and technologies to make those opportunities realities.

Chapter Six provides an overview of enterprise architecture (EA). EA is an important planning process that IT often leads, but that should be made transparent to the rest of the company. The strategic plans across the organization should translate into business architecture, data architecture, application architecture, and systems or IT architecture. The fit of the new into the old should be contemplated. Those things that create redundancy in the architecture should be retired or sunsetted. Most important, the EA must remain up to date, and aligning it with the strategic planning process is the way to ensure that it is.

Chapter Seven provides an overview on how best to review, refresh, and communicate plans. It is all well and good to create a strategic plan, but a plan is only as good as the company's ability to execute it. This requires clear and cogent communications that make it real for people at all levels of the company. It should also be disseminated quickly so that the entire division or company receives word nearly at the same time.

By the time you reach the conclusion of the book in Chapter Eight, you will have a comprehensive view of strategic planning, led by the CIO and IT executive team. Your company may be more or less mature. This book has something for executives no matter the profile. You may read some chapters faster as a result of your division or company doing some of these aspects well already. Others may require lingering over to a greater extent. Either way, I hope you'll find that the path to demonstrably better IT and ultimately company performance lies in the methods I will describe.

2

The CIO as Strategic Facilitator

Who sets the priorities for your IT department? In many cases, it can seem that it is the leaders of other parts of the organization without ample push-back from IT. Whose fault is that, however?

The role of CIOs is a thankless one in many ways. They and their leadership teams receive a wide variety of input from the rest of the organization in a wide variety of ways. Requests may come through casual conversation, email, or an impromptu phone call. Some divisions may produce planning documents the size of phone books. Others may use only a single page. Often the expectation from the executives outside of IT is that these conversations are directing work for the IT department, not necessarily recognizing that IT must balance the priorities of all divisions of the organization in order to come up with its own one-to-n ranked priority of projects. In successful companies, growth of the company leads to growth of demand for new technology, exacerbating the pressure on IT. Something has to give.

Part of the problem is that many companies are better at corporate strategy than they are at divisional or business unit strategy. The reasons for this are many, but often divisional heads focus more on execution than on planning. Not translating corporate strategy into divisional strategy means that the company's strategy is half-baked at best. In this situation, it is natural that other divisions' guidance to IT will come in as various touchpoints rather than through clear plans against which IT can map its activities, let alone contribute suggestions to make the plans more comprehensive and valuable.

Typically in situations like this, the executives outside of IT will not identify this issue or volunteer a solution. IT executives themselves must diagnose the problem and let it be known that IT operates better when it has maximum clarity from each of the divisions in the form of well-articulated plans that provide guidance on priorities and on what the future is likely to hold from each division's perspective, and the longer the time horizon the better. IT operates best when those plans are issued with a common level of clarity and a common level of granularity, hopefully with success metrics providing further guidance. Unfortunately, this is rarely the case. However, there is something that CIOs can do about it.

In this chapter, I will show how, rather than being the target of other divisions' vague or unprioritized demands, IT itself should and can become a center for promoting a coordinated, well-thought-out program of strategies for the company as a whole and each of its separate divisions. My main example for this chapter is Jo-ann Olsovsky, CIO of BNSF Railway. Promoted to that spot from assistant vice president of telecommunications, she became the head of IT of an organization that, dating back to 1849, is one of the largest railroads in the United States, and incredibly successful.

Clarity About Priorities

When Olsovsky stepped in as CIO in June of 2008, the company's demand for IT was increasing, as many of its strategic projects as well as the projects mandated by the government were being brought to life through technology.

BNSF Railway has long been one of the strongest companies in the world from an operational perspective. At its core it is a major logistics operation, for instance, identifying cargo that enters a seaport in Los Angeles, loading it onto a rail car from a ship, hauling it across the country, and oftentimes engaging a vast array of trucking partners to take the cargo over the "last mile" of delivery direct to a customer. Freight loads might include consumer electronics, coal, oil, food, or a variety of other goods on which the American economy is founded. This logistical and operational strength is at the core of BNSF's success.

BNSF's track record had been enviable, and as the company continued to grow, demand for IT's systems and services continued apace. When Olsovsky stepped in, IT's resources and budget had not grown to the same extent. In the face of this limitation, she knew it was important to get greater clarity from and for the rest of the organization so that she could ensure that top priorities were first to be addressed. Also, increasingly important was a need to create a linkage between the strategic plans from the divisions of the company (Operations, Finance, Marketing, Human Resources, and so on) and IT itself. The paramount need was an enterprise-wide, multiyear view of technology. What IT stood to gain from such linkage was a clearer perspective on its conundrum of demand outpacing IT's supply of resources.

Engaging Divisional Leaders and Strategies

Olsovsky and her team engaged the leaders of each of the divisions and embarked on an exercise to more fully understand the plans of each as well as to understand the current business processes and systems as they interconnect. The goal was not just to be able to ensure that IT was directionally correct in its technology investment on behalf of each of those divisions, but also to give IT insight into how to drive competitive differentiators and business efficiency via the systems modernization and implementations that would be under way.

Under Olsovsky's watch as part of the annual planning cycle, the technology team works to understand the business direction, current challenges, risks, and so on from both the business and the technology points of view. Business objectives are documented and are then translated to technology objectives. This does not mean that a division's strategic plans need to be rewritten or redirected in some dramatic way. In some cases, it does mean recasting existing technology plans with more accessible language so that people outside of the division can more clearly understand the direction suggested by the plans, can suggest enhancements to them, and can align their own efforts to them where appropriate and in such a way that the employees chartered with executing do understand the true business drivers.

Seeing Commonalities

At a higher level of importance, engagement with the divisions put Olsovsky's IT team in a position to read across the plans of different divisions to begin to uncover themes about which IT needed to develop perspectives. Immature IT departments treat the relationship with each business unit or division of the company as an independent set of conversations and planning exercises without contemplating the commonalities and differences among these plans. Yet IT is one of the few parts of an organization that can and should identify commonalities, teasing out the needs of each division, optimally with each leader present, so that each hears the objectives of the others and can suggest additions or subtractions from those plans or from their own plans. Once commonalities are noted, IT is better positioned to identify a single solution that will address common or similar needs of the divisions.

Clarity About Ownership Costs

Olsovsky removed the opaqueness of IT's plans of the past and made them more transparent. After all, the clarity IT is after is not just for itself but for the divisional leaders as well. Along these lines, the CIO's peer leaders need to realize that the cost of managing IT projects does not cease when projects are implemented. A software product, whether created by internal resources or purchased "off the shelf" from a vendor, requires maintenance and potential upgrades, and must be integrated and potentially reintegrated as other software products interact with it. All this requires IT time and effort—time and effort that will not be available for new development. Therefore, the total cost of ownership of each IT investment must be evaluated, and the long-term time and cost ramifications of each decision must be highlighted at the earliest possible stage. Business cases should always include the total cost of ownership as a key financial metric, and therefore a key decision-making criterion.

Trendspotting

IT departments should also lead the way in noticing trends related to technology and how those trends might serve new partnerships between various divisions of the organization.

How can a CIO recognize cues from conversations and interactions with peer leaders to understand where IT might be helpful? It begins with regular, informal interactions with executives across the company to complement more formal interactions that the strategic planning process might entail, but it also means remaining abreast of trends to push the thinking of these leaders, or to more readily identify where a need or an opportunity articulated by another leader might be met with an investment in the areas defined by the trends.

In recent years, some of the key trends and opportunities that IT departments and their companies more generally have focused on a great deal have included

- Social and mobile network interactions
- Consumerization of IT
- Advanced data analytics
- Virtualization and cloud computing

Figure 2.1 shows some of the potential partnering around needs and plans related to each of these trends. The figure is not

Trend	Potential Partners
Social and Mobile Network Interactions	• Marketing • Public Relations and Communications • Human Resources • Legal • External customers • eCommerce
Consumerization of IT	• Human Resources • Legal • Information security • Risk management • External customers
Advanced Analytics	• Operations • Finance • Procurement • Marketing • Sales
Virtualization and Cloud Computing	• Product Development • Engineering

Figure 2.1. Some Recent Trends and Potential Partners.

exhaustive but represents a way of thinking and illustrates how opportunities from these and other technology trends are relevant not just to IT but to other constituents as well. By identifying and discussing trends like these with other divisions, IT can further promote coordination overall.

An IT They Can't Leave Out

I've begun to speak of partnering, but let's consider the possibility that some other parts of the organization may not wish to partner with IT. This is often the case when potential partners perceive that

IT is not responsive to their clear and present needs. In these conditions, so called "rogue IT" operations may crop up. Consumerization of IT is a great example of a range of topics for which there is a perception that it may be best to exclude IT. For instance, the Marketing department may wish to develop an app for its customers. In some cases, not a great deal of effort may be required to develop something that customers will use. Marketing may decide to pursue this without directly involving the IT team, or even believing that it would be better for IT simply not to know about the initiative. Many cloud and software-as-a-service vendors have effectively sold their wares to executives other than the CIO, intentionally bypassing the IT department. Such moves speak volumes about an unhealthy relationship between other departments and IT.

Other examples can be much more deleterious. If the Sales division elects to invest in an analytics platform, it may be wooed by a vendor's promise that the platform can be implemented cheaply and easily. Sales leaders may feel so compelled that they elect not to consult IT. Most analytics platforms—whether they are used to assess potential client opportunities, opportunities to sell additional products or services to existing clients, or other purposes— are likely to be at least moderately complex, and it is *highly* likely that IT will soon need to support the technology and interact with the vendor, since few Sales divisions have the kinds of resources to do so. When CIOs begin to see these sorts of decisions being made without their involvement, it is time to worry about the state of their relationship with other divisions.

IT: An Indispensable Consultant and Facilitator

IT leaders should aspire to be indispensable in these sorts of decisions. Far from getting in the way or slowing down the process, they should be thought of as internal consultants who will help weigh the pros and cons of each contemplated vendor or technology. IT should provide perspectives that the other divisions had not thought of. For example, IT needs to explain the need to keep an up-to-date infrastructure roadmap and enterprise architecture map reflecting the plans and projects of each division of the company, so that there is always a comprehensive and transparent view of the company's current and planned technology.

When IT is the indispensable consultant to each of the company's divisions, IT's value to the organization as a whole begins to multiply further. As I mentioned earlier, IT is ideally suited to understand where there are themes that emerge from across the organization. Look again at Figure 2.1, especially the four potential partner divisions (Operations, Procurement, Marketing, and Sales) whose needs relate to advanced analytics. The CIO and the IT leadership team should be there, as close as possible to the divisions when divisional plans are still being hatched and are still open to influence and change. IT leaders may well be the first to recognize that there is a common need across the four divisions; that being so, the CIO should chair a conversation among the leaders of the four. Leaders from each division may enter the meeting thinking that their needs are unique. In a Venn diagram, for example, they might imagine that the circle representing their needs overlaps very little with any other division's circle. This is regularly the assumption at the outset of these conversations, but it is rarely the conclusion coming out of them. Already attuned to commonalities itself, IT is well suited to facilitate the conversations to help the leaders of each division recognize them, too. In so doing, IT positions itself as a source of collaboration from across the corporation, a source of efficiency, through which a single or short list of solutions may be identified to address most of the needs of the divisions. If this is known early, IT will understand early what solutions it will need to support.

IT will also be in a good position to call out to the same leaders about where it sees articulated needs diverging or conflicting across the organization. Before investments must be made, IT will understand where solutions will be redundant, as is so often the case in organizations in which IT does not have a sufficient handle on the investments early in the process. The fewer the number of solutions invested in, the lower the complexity of the IT footprint, and the easier time a CIO will have of managing IT. In the chapters that follow, we will explore these concepts in greater detail, and in Chapter Four I will describe processes to guide these conversations about strategy and solutions at the corporate and divisional levels.

Early Intervention into Planning

BNSF CIO Jo-ann Olsovsky recognized both the opportunity to integrate her team earlier into the planning process of leaders across the organization and the advantage of increasing the transparency of plans and projects introduced by IT and by the rest of the organization.

Focus on Business Rather Than Technology Questions

Olsovsky and her team began with a series of conversations with each of the divisional leaders and their direct reports. The conversations were about where the divisions envisioned heading in the foreseeable future. The IT team posed questions such as

- What strengths does your division have that need to be exploited?
- What are the areas that you would like to see improved?
- How do we see our business evolving in the next three to five years?
- Where can we drive efficiency between internal departments?
- How can we improve customer stickiness?
- How can we improve service?
- How can we improve responsiveness and agility?
- How do we stack up in comparison with our competitors?

Questions like these got the ball rolling, and many other questions followed. Notice that these are not IT questions. If she and her team had asked strictly IT questions (for example, "What new technology do you think you need in the foreseeable future?"), they would have been asking divisional spokespeople to pose as experts in the area in which she and her team were the real experts. It also would have limited the conversation, and would not have generated such a richness of insights.

In many ways, these are questions a consultant would ask, and therefore Olsovsky's team was acting as internal consultants. The effect of that was that when divisions identified internal projects to improve their operating processes, they asked IT to be part of their team. That is one of the ways in which IT leaders should think about their jobs.

Draw Upon the Strengths of Consultants

Traits of good consultants include the following:

- They are curious.
- They are great listeners.
- They observe independent units and create linkages with end-to-end processes.
- They spend time embedded and observing day-to-day business operations.
- They ask great questions that allow for deeper explorations of issues or needs.
- They are comfortable when faced with issues that have uncertain paths to resolution—in fact, they often thrive in such situations.
- They develop thought-provoking research into best practices, as well as draw examples from comparable companies that are not necessarily competitors.
- They develop hypotheses, but take a data-driven approach to validate or disprove those hypotheses.

CIOs and IT leaders generally should push themselves and their teams to adopt these characteristics to drive positive change for the rest of the organization.

Become Transparent

Related to deeper involvement in divisional planning, another important attribute of the successful modern IT executive is to render the IT organization transparent. This transparency should apply to IT's budget, the value it is returning for that budget, its performance relative to a variety of performance metrics, and its plans. IT has historically been a black box to the rest of the organization, not clearly understood by many. Unfortunately, this lack of understanding has been a source of shortsighted personal power to IT leaders, as they have often been the only people who truly understand their domain. In such a position they are not often pressed to make the case to prove the value of their projects with a return-on-investment analysis. Not expecting such a thing causes other leaders to perceive even more the "otherness" of the IT division: a cost center whose cost management is obscure and esoteric.

Figure 2.2 gives some insight into the history of this opaque "otherness" of IT and how the Internet has forced it toward the light of day. For decades, IT managed a variety of things that were not at all understood by the rest of the organization. That changed in the mid-1990s with the Internet revolution, ushered in by the Netscape IPO in August of 1995. All of a sudden many traditional businesses had competition that did not have stores and barely had offices. Savvy old businesses began to seize this opportunity as well, developing eBusiness channels. With these changes, IT was viewed and began to operate in a different light. The pace of this revolution has only increased since then with the emergence of wireless devices, social networks, cloud-based offerings, and ultimately the Internet of things, in which sensors embedded in objects communicate through networks, providing data that computers analyze. Now businesses ignore IT at their own peril, and this recognition has meant that

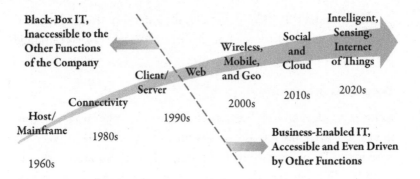

Figure 2.2.   The Internet Revolution and the Coming-Out of IT.

non-IT executives have had to become much more IT savvy. This has brought on invitations for the savviest IT executives to become advisors to the rest of the organization.

Olsovsky's IT Strategy

Olsovsky understood the opportunity we've just described. As she continued strategy conversations with her colleagues, she developed an IT roadmap with a common level of clarity and granularity that was aligned with the divisions' objectives, which allowed the IT department to see trends and themes that were emerging from across the company. That alignment provided powerful insights that only an executive who has reason to collaborate with a cross-section of the corporation can derive. She highlighted ten themes or objectives that she summarized as the "Business of IT" (see Figure 2.3). These were imperatives of the business in which IT had a role to push it forward. She called this overall IT strategy "RailRoad 2020" to signal a perspective aiming several years out.

Once the "Business of IT" objectives were defined, it was important to develop complementary technology objectives. Of these, she named the four approvals in Figure 2.4.

1. Customer
2. Service
3. Asset
4. Workforce
5. Corporate services
6. Positioning for Railroad 2020
7. Get native with the rail business
8. Deliver faster
9. Break out of the 80/20 spending trap; think total cost of ownership
10. Build the bench

Figure 2.3. RailRoad 2020 IT Strategy—"Business of IT" Objectives.

1. Available
2. Modernize
3. Mobile
4. Intelligent

Figure 2.4. RailRoad 2020 IT Strategy—Technology Objectives.

In this way Olsovsky answered the question of whether business strategy and IT strategy are one and the same or two different things. I agree: they are best described as two sides of the same coin.

Both sets of objectives look to the future. That said, every IT department must also continue to manage what it already has implemented. As Olsovsky noted, "Good IT operating practices still apply. You can't look to the future without continuing to manage the present."[1] Therefore, she defined ten operating practices, shown in Figure 2.5.

Olsovsky directed her team not to be the order takers, as so many IT leaders have been in IT departments of the past and unfortunately still are today. Yes, the leaders of Operations, Marketing,

1. Eliminate unnecessary complexity
2. Standardize and simplify the architecture
3. Eliminate redundancy
4. Buy versus build; use and reuse
5. Find and eliminate noise*
6. Reduce mean time to recovery and identify root cause
7. Ensure highly available, diverse, and redundant critical systems and failover capability
8. Measure and improve performance
9. Leverage IP and open standard technologies
10. Take advantage of advanced technologies

Figure 2.5. Olsovsky's Operating Practices.

*Noise refers to those things that cause outages and service disruption, thus distracting IT engineers from delivering proactive strategic work and instead wasting time without delivering any real benefit.

Finance, HR, and other divisions of the organization are experts in their fields, but, as Olsovsky says,

> It is our charter to learn their challenges; however we must determine the technology solutions to apply to them. It is in our mission to be good stewards of the technology investments we deploy. Therefore, we must be prudent investors for the long haul, looking at the business cross-functionally versus being wasteful by customizing systems that, in the end, drive total cost of ownership higher and create a longer-term problem.

I believe Olsovsky's story should translate to other CIOs, no matter the industry. In any private or public organization, the CIO should hold strategic conversations and use them to help other parts of the organization to align and to create a supportive IT strategy.

Introducing the OGTM

There are many strategy models, and terms overlap from one to another. Strategies, goals, objectives, priorities, plans—the words are interchanged, with different models arranging them in different hierarchical orders. Various models are workable, but within an organization it is important that plans be developed in a language which is consistent. IT leaders need to encourage the rest of the organization to share one format so that comparisons can be made easily across plans. It is remarkable how often plans are not consistently rendered, but as I noted before, the more inconsistency there is across plans, the more difficult it becomes for the CIO and the IT leadership team to interpret these plans to prioritize the work of IT. Whatever model you can agree on, push for this consistency.

In this book, I will provide examples of several strategy models. For consistency within this book, most often I will use the framework that my firm, Metis Strategy, uses with the clients we advise. We refer to it as OGTM, which is short for "objectives, goals, tactics, and measures." The following describes how we define the terms.

> *Objectives.* An objective is any one of the corporation's or division's overarching pursuits for the next three to five years. It is important that these be developed with a long time horizon in mind. At the corporate level, objectives tend to relate to revenue growth, cost-cutting, geographic expansion, acquisitions, customer satisfaction, and the like. Often missing, however, is translation of these broad objectives to language that has clear meaning for each of the separate divisions of the corporation. That is an important omission because large corporate objectives tend not to offer much of a filtering mechanism or means of bringing divisions into alignment. This is key because a strategic plan needs to be as much about what the organization should *not* do as about what it should.

By and large, because objectives should help provide focus to the organization, fewer are better than many. If a company has fifteen objectives, for instance, it is not likely to have a great sense of where to focus its attention. Almost any proposed project may easily fit by the criteria of *some* objective. The less the company is focused, the less it will succeed.

Goals. OGTM uses this term to mean metrics of success. As metrics, goals should be fashioned as means of qualifying success at achieving an objective. Each goal needs to be SMART, an acronym that means

- Specific
- Measurable
- Actionable
- Realistic
- Time-constrained[2]

The number of goals should be limited so that they will serve as effective foci. As with objectives, the more goals there are, the less effectively they filter.

Tactics. Tactics are the actions that the company or division might undertake in order to accomplish the objective and goal(s). The list of possible tactics should be unconstrained in the brainstorming phase; the more the merrier. Only after that phase should tactics be winnowed and ranked, based on the ability of each to drive accomplishment of the objective and goal(s).

Measures. The relationship between a measure and a tactic is akin to the relationship between a goal and an objective. Like a goal, a measure is a metric, but one that is used to gauge the success of a particular tactic rather than broader success on an objective. That which gets measured gets done, so having both goals and measures provides the motivation for all involved to ensure progress is being made, and to ensure that corrective action is taken when needed.

Objective	Goals (Objective Key Performance Indicators, or KPIs)
The corporation's or division's overarching pursuits for the next three to five years	The quantifiable metric that determines the degree to which an objective has been successfully reached
Tactics	Measures (Tactic KPIs)
The various actions available to a company that will help the company reach its goals	The quantifiable metric that determines the degree to which a tactic has been accomplished

Figure 2.6. Metis Strategy's Strategy Model: OGTM.

Figure 2.6 summarizes OGTM. What you see in the figure becomes essentially a masthead to a document containing more detailed information, as I will explain in Chapter Four.

What Makes IT So Inherently Strategic?

You may be thinking, "This seems like a general strategic framework, rather than an IT-specific strategic framework." Right you are! IT is a business function and, as such, should use the same methodology as the rest of the organization. The structure of the OGTM will be highlighted throughout the book as one for CEOs, division heads, and IT leaders alike. In fact, the best and most logical cascade of the OGTMs will be in that order. Optimally, the CEO has multiple OGTMs (for each of the several objectives the CEO considers imperative for the foreseeable future); the division heads compose their own OGTMs linked to those of the CEO. Ideally, an IT leader goes last in preparing IT's OGTMs, after the CIO has participated in strategy-setting conversations with each of the rest of the corporate leaders. Only at that point can the CIO best determine how to focus IT's limited resources. Chapter Four and the following chapters in this book go further into the practicalities of enacting

and supporting the overall cascade. For companies that have immature strategy-setting processes, Chapter Four delves into how the
CIO should work with the CEO and the division leaders to create
OGTMs in each case. As I will note elsewhere herein, sometimes
the CIO will have to make the first move, mocking up a strategic
plan in concert with an open-minded peer who heads another division. In other cases, the IT OGTM will have to come first, and,
again, IT can set an example that other divisions can follow.

Ultimately, the tactics and measures at the corporate level
should translate into and align with the objectives and goals of
the divisions. Some but not all of IT's objectives and goals will
align with the corporate tactics and measures. Other IT objectives
and goals will develop in service of divisional tactics and measures.
IT is an advisor and provider of services to both the corporation
at large and the rest of the divisions, and should be documented
as such. Figure 2.7 distills these alignments into a chart that
summarizes where IT sits within the overall "strategic cascade."
It may seem a little confusing at first that IT is present in both the
second and third columns. As we revisit this chart repeatedly in
later chapters, applying it to concrete examples, that duplication

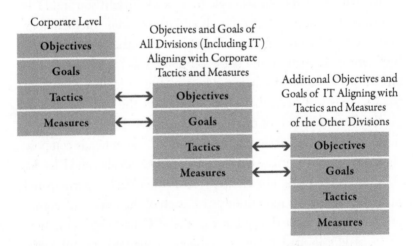

Figure 2.7. IT's Alignment within an Overall OGTM Cascade.

will no longer seem confusing, and the chart will make more and more sense.

The Value of Boldness

This following chapters provide examples for executives whose companies have little by way of true strategic plans, and for those who already get some strategic guidance from the CEO and the division heads but have not yet appropriately and effectively translated those strategies through to IT. I also believe they can be used for strategically mature companies looking for a tighter process to use to revalidate plans. As I will emphasize later in the book at greater length, the IT leader has not traditionally been the executive who has pushed for more strategic clarity from the rest of the organization, but the fact that IT must be inserted at multiple levels in Figure 2.7 points out its potential to be one of the most strategic functions in the company. As such, any lack of strategic clarity on the part of the rest of the organization will have a unique impact on IT, I argue, and that impact will be negative. Therefore, the CIO should be emboldened to appropriately push his or her colleagues to provide clear plans. In return, the CIO will be better positioned to suggest where there are opportunities for more collaboration across the company. It is time for CIOs to be bold!

As I mentioned, Chapter Four will take us into a CIO's role in facilitating corporate and divisional strategy. In Chapter Three, however, we'll highlight how IT may need to reframe its basic sense of mission to break out of older limiting habits. In fact, as corporations clarify and claim their missions, so I urge IT departments to do the same.

Take-Aways on IT's Central Role in Strategy

1. Be bold, and do not wait for the change that you have identified as necessary. Be that change!

2. IT's resources are limited. Make it your goal that your IT department will set its own clear priorities, based on what corporate and divisions need from you in order to pursue their highest priorities.

3. Become the company's eyes and ears for short- and longer-term trends in technology and its business uses.

4. Take the initiative to engage divisional leaders in early talks about their planning of objectives and goals.

   • Focus on their needs and perspectives.

   • Ask them questions about business, not about technology (your area of expertise).

   • Find commonalities in what various divisions are trying to do and focus resources on common themes.

5. Host partnering conversations across divisions that are based on their needs and your knowledge of technological means and trends.

6. Notice who is leaving IT out of the loop in technology matters. See that as a sign of a poor relationship between you both. Explore the root cause of the problem and show why everyone is better off when IT is in the loop.

7. Work toward consulting and facilitating roles with peers in other divisions. Cultivate your consulting skills.

8. Make IT more transparent regarding its costs and financial value. Analyze and report IT's ROI.

9. Build strategy for IT.

   • Begin with long-term business concerns and objectives based on talks with divisions.

   • Construct business objectives specifically for IT.

   • Translate the IT business objectives into a short list of technology objectives.

- Define and attend to ongoing operating practices that IT must maintain right now.

10. Advocate for a unifying strategy language and model that Corporate and all divisions can use and support.

11. Cultivate an IT attitude of more proactive partnerships, less "taking orders."

3

IT Missions

I'd like to tell a story about a friend of mine who is a CIO, whom I'll call "Jerry." He is the CIO of a multibillion dollar technology firm. When Jerry joined the firm, he began to ask other members of the leadership team about their plans and found out they didn't have much. At best, what had been produced (by Marketing, Finance, Human Resources, Sales, Engineering, and even at the level of the CEO of the company) was tactical rather than strategic.

One CIO's Filtered Vision

Jerry's new firm suffered from a common ailment among fast-growing companies that have not reached anywhere near saturation in their markets: their number one objective is to "increase sales." Sales targets might be better defined as, "Increase by 25 percent in the next fiscal year," but if those targets aren't qualified further, their suggestion is that *any* new revenue is *good* revenue. What the target doesn't say is, for example,

> *What's the targeted profitability of the new revenue?* Do we go after revenue growth that might deteriorate the current rate of profitability?
>
> *Should revenue growth derive from existing products and services or from new products and services?* People in general, especially sales teams, have a tendency to revert to pushing what they know versus what they do not, and so without clear guidance,

the tendency will be to continue to push existing products and services.

Should revenue growth come through existing channels, customers, or geographies, as opposed to revenue from new channels, customers, or geographies? Again, what is known is likely to be pushed more than the new and unknown, so it's important to declare where new channels should be leveraged, which new customers to target, and which new geographies to enter.

Should revenue growth be organic, or can we grow it by acquiring another company? Each of these is a noble way to grow revenue, and some companies are better suited to acquiring companies than others. Nevertheless, we need to know how these factors should be taken into consideration.

There are other factors to consider, but as is an ongoing theme in this book, the more general the objective, the fewer ideas will be filtered along the way. Filters are essential to planning. I will reiterate: strategy is as much about defining what *not* to do as it is about what to do. Declaring the sanctity of sales growth (an essential objective, of course) without qualifying the type of revenue growth that one should attempt to achieve does not provide an adequate filter, which in turn means the organization will lack focus. With a dearth of filters in his firm, Jerry realized that he was not likely to get the level of granularity and clarity he required in order to help IT develop its own strategy with full confidence that these plans could be woven together.

No "Internal Customers" of IT

Facing Jerry's situation, a great number of CIOs would simply keep their heads down and continue to take direction from their colleagues outside of IT, not challenging the status quo. These are passive CIOs who have reconciled themselves to being vendors to the business. Incidentally, these often are also the leaders who refer to the rest of the organization as "customers," a subservient language that speaks volumes and declares a great distance between IT and the true customers: those consumers, businesses, or both that actually provide the revenue for the company. It practically admits that the IT department will have nothing to do with actual customers. Also, as the axiom suggests, "the customer is always right," so when colleagues are thought of as "customers," a CIO is not likely to push back when they make requests with which the CIO disagrees, or the CIO will not raise concerns as they arise. It is important that IT recognize that *the only customers are those people who provide funds to the company*, and refer to colleagues as, well, colleagues or perhaps as partners.

You will also note that I try to avoid referring to "the business" as something that is separate from IT. It is still quite common for CIOs to refer to the rest of the organization as "the business," but again it suggests a distance between what it does and where true business value is created. The IT team must think of itself as part of the business. Therefore, I like to refer to "IT and the rest of the organization," and to the CIO and his or her colleagues in other divisions as "the IT team and colleagues outside of IT." Words matter, and this is a message I have been hammering home with my CIO clients extensively for the past few years.

Projects Don't Drive Strategy

Jerry is bold—not a status quo leader. As he asked his colleagues in IT simple questions about how IT had generated the list of projects it was working on, and how the projects were prioritized, the answers he got were unclear. The typical response went something like this: "One of the functional heads spoke with the CIO [Jerry's predecessor] about the latest critical project that needed to be given top priority. At the time, we were working on what the same executive had indicated earlier was the most crucial project, but that didn't seem to matter."

These kinds of seemingly arbitrary turnabouts were common-
place, and there was no strategy in place to refocus the conversation.
Priorities should change at times, of course, in the face of factors
such as

- Changes in the economic outlook
- Changes forged by a competitor that require a response
- A natural disaster having an impact on a part of the
  operation
- Legal action against the company
- The failure or success of a product or service launch
- The departure of a leader
- Identification of new market opportunities that are under-
  served by competitors
- Revelation of new data or prototypes that necessitate a pivot
- The acquisition or divestiture of a business

Changes in priorities should drive changes in projects, not the
other way around. In reality, often project ideas are allowed to trump
strategy, and the opinions of a single, powerful executive trump the
logic of the strategic plan.

The consequences of this inconsistency can be negative in several ways. First, it leads to confusion and frustration among those
people who were working on a high-priority project who now must
stop and change to a different high-priority project. It is only natural
that people who spend time working on a project would like to see
it through to success. When the rug is yanked out from under them,
the team does not see its projects reaching fruition and feels unful-
filled inasmuch as they've wasted their time. If a decision for this
sort of change happens without a strategic plan in place that offers
objective criteria to explain why a change is necessary, then the
apparent arbitrariness of the decision only adds to the frustration.

This is unfortunate because members of a team that is frustrated due to the change may well be the same people who need to drive the new initiative. Frustrate the team too regularly, and you sap the energy of some of your most important employees and dilute their efforts on whatever is next.

Jerry's conclusion after investigating these issues was that IT lacked a clear strategy of its own. Much of this was due to the fact that the rest of the organization was not clear as to where the business should be in one or three or five years, and no one was offering thoughts on the processes, products, and services that would get them there other than simple extensions of what already existed. Jerry recognized all of these issues, and also realized that if IT failed to deliver, even though part of that failure was due to a lack of strategic direction on the part of the rest of the organization, he would be to blame. For the sake of his team, as well as for the sake of self-preservation, Jerry chose a different path.

Mission Time

Given a lack of a strategy from the rest of the organization, Jerry elected to create a mission for his IT department to follow. While not a full-fledged IT strategy, the mission would declare for his team, for himself, and to his colleagues a "true north" of sorts that IT would align with. If a project arose, the team would have a single filter to use to help determine whether the team should proceed or not.

As a single-phrase filter, the mission statement would be imperfect, and broader than a multipoint strategy. Still, it would provide some interim filtering. It would be a starting point that could also be used as a conversation starter as he hoped to coax the rest of the organization to develop plans.

The process of creating a mission also was energizing for Jerry's leadership team. Prior to an initial mission session, he had each person reach out to the constituents outside of IT that they knew best to let them know that IT was holding a planning session in order to create an IT mission. This act alone yielded interesting insights from the rest of the organization regarding plans, even if they were not articulated as full-blown strategies. For instance,

- Some leaders outside IT wanted IT to develop more customer-facing technologies. This came as a pleasant surprise for some in IT who thought that the rest of the organization viewed IT as a function that focused only internally.

- Several executives from the rest of the organization recognized that IT touched all divisions in ways that other divisions did not, and so Jerry's staff were counseled to be bold in identifying business processes that could be rendered more efficient using technology. Members of the IT team were also pushed to identify business processes that could be improved, consolidated, or eliminated.

From this input, Jerry developed the following mission:

Leverage technology to improve business processes and operations to benefit our company and our customers.

Deconstructing Jerry's IT Mission

By dissecting Jerry's IT mission, we can understand what Jerry hoped to accomplish.

"Leverage technology . . ." The mission statement acknowledged that "technology" is IT's purview and thus the domain it can leverage.

". . . Improve business processes and operations . . ." Jerry realized that IT is one of the few parts of an organization (sometimes the only one) that interacts with most if not all business processes in one way or another. As such, IT sees the business operations from the front end to the back end, and acts as the central nervous

system of the organization. Therefore, IT should be charged with identifying ways to automate existing processes, but also to harmonize and optimize processes.

As an organizational choice (though not one Jerry opted to make), a number of IT departments are choosing to set up their organizational chart on the basis of business processes rather than aligning them to standard IT activities (development, infrastructure, quality assurance, and so on), business functions, geographies, or the like. For example, among other alignments, IT can align to a process such as "order to cash," meaning the chain of events starting when a customer places an order and ending at the point at which cash is collected and revenue is recognized. This process is relevant to every revenue-earning division of the company, and for some companies and industries, the lag between order placed and revenue banked can be substantial. Creative use of automation may shave valuable days or even weeks off the process. To the extent that IT can develop and automate better processes across the organization, can suggest process consolidation so that multiple divisions leverage the same processes when appropriate, and can enable these processes with automation, IT can be the glue that brings the company closer together, rendering efficiencies while also stimulating collaboration in some surprising ways.

Too many CIOs decide to purchase or build solutions without thinking about the people and process points first. Sorting out the latter two items first before committing to a technology is critical. Jerry's vision was not grand enough in the area of process improvement to warrant changing his organizational chart but, nevertheless, he recognized a need for IT to align its activities to business processes, as a key layer of value.

". . . *To benefit our company* . . ." Jerry's statement pointed out that he intended information technology to benefit the company. This suggests that metrics should be put in place to gauge value derived from IT. That value may come in the form of greater productivity, improved cost efficiencies, or better decision making based on more timely availability of data, just to name three layers of value.

"... *And our customers*..." IT departments have not held the true customer in their purview nearly as much as they should. The neglect is exacerbated by the fact I mentioned earlier, that many IT departments refer to colleagues as "customers." Jerry was sure to emphasize the need to focus on true customers as part of the mission.

From Source of Insight to Substance of Message

Much of the logic expressed in Jerry's IT mission occurred to its makers only in the act of making it. Once the IT leadership team agreed to it, he made sure that each member of the team truly bought into the mission and would tell his or her teams about it, pass on the logic that led to its creation, and use the statement as a way of gauging whether ideas they pursued were focused appropriately.

The creation of the IT mission also armed Jerry with a message to bring to his peers in the leadership team of the company. Previously he hadn't had the guidance that he needed from the rest of the leaders; in the absence of clear plans from them, he could say that his team would use the IT mission as the first screen to gauge the validity of the portfolio of activities that IT would undertake.

Jerry's colleagues outside of IT were impressed by the proactive approach that he undertook. As some of them probed to determine what strategy was in place to support this IT mission, it provided Jerry with the opening he needed to engage the rest of the organization in a conversation about the need for clearer plans. Had he done so without having taken a first step himself, his request might have seemed hollow. Since no mission existed in other parts of the organization, Jerry could claim the moral high ground and have a productive conversation requesting comparable clarity elsewhere, having taken the first step.

Let's move on to two more examples of inventing an IT mission, at Google and Marriott.

IT Mission at Google

One might think that being the CIO of a legendary technology company would be like *A Tale of Two Cities*: the best of times and the worst of times. On one hand, at a company such as Google one need not ever make the case that technology needs to be thought of as a strategic weapon in the arsenal of the company, as many IT executives still must do in their companies. On the other hand, there are many people throughout the business who feel they can do the job of CIO better than can the actual CIO. For many of the company's engineers, CIO seems like the easiest of the executive positions.

Google CIO Ben Fried's job is far from easy, but he focuses more on the best-of-times scenario, recognizing that by being surrounded by some of the best technology talent in the world inside and outside the IT department, he has no dearth of opportunities to pursue. In fact, even the issues turn out to be opportunities. As he says, "At Google, we are programmed to think that if you see an opportunity or a problem, we need to do something about it."

When Fried joined Google in May of 2008 after more than thirteen years at Morgan Stanley, there were a great number of opportunities to chase down and a good number of issues to resolve. This is typical for an organization that has been through such tremendous growth as Google had. The company's core services (such as Search, Gmail, YouTube, and Maps) have grown tremendously, and the company continues to grow through acquisition. The complexity is exacerbated and the opportunities multiplied by the company's continued desire to shoot for the moon with ideas such as Google Glass or the driverless cars emerging out of Google X. Fried's team's ability to react quickly to these opportunities earned it a reputation for being experts with the tactics.

They could seize upon an opportunity or squelch a problem as soon as either was identified.

A couple of years ago, Fried wanted to plant a figurative flag to declare what Google IT stood for. As the company continued its tremendous growth, the demands on IT would grow accordingly, and without a filter to allow it to prioritize, the department might be crushed under the weight of the growing needs and expectations of the rest of the organization.

Fried and his leadership team defined Google IT's mission:

To empower Googlers with world leading technology.

(*Googlers* is the term that Google employees use to describe themselves.)

This is a bold statement, clearly asserting that average is not good enough. If that seems too bold, consider that the company's mission as a whole is "To organize the world's information and make it universally accessible and useful." The IT mission grew out of that because one ambitious mission deserves another to support it. At least three implications are noteworthy about the Google IT mission.

First, it requires that IT develop tight collaborations with colleagues outside of IT, so that the department truly knows what Googlers need to be successful. Fried had a valuable arrow in his quiver: he had some of the deepest engineering talent in the world, and in many cases his team could seek the counsel of colleagues who had invented significant aspects of the Internet, technology infrastructure, and computer languages. That said, at the time Fried's team defined its mission, IT needed to develop stronger ties with these experts earlier on in the development of new technologies.

In line with this theme of collaboration, like other executives Fried encourages his team to think of their workspaces as fluid. Individuals tend not to have fixed spaces, but rather gather in clusters that are emblematic of the collaborations that are necessary for whatever topic or project is currently being pursued. On one of my trips to Fried's New York office, members of the IT team occupied office space with members of the product law department on the basis of project ideas that required the expertise of each, as an example.

The second implication of the mission is that IT would eschew following others and instead lean toward developing the truly new. For many companies, infrastructure would not be counted as truly new and innovative. Many companies think of it as a commodity to be outsourced. At Google, infrastructure is a source of competitive advantage. Google has a liberal policy in allowing employees to choose the technology they need, and Fried and team make sure that the infrastructure backbone is strong enough to ensure that Googlers' experience is flawless no matter the technology that they use.

Fried has also been a key catalyst in Google's efforts to provide free wi-fi hotspots in a number of cities, including in the Chelsea neighborhood of New York where Google's East Coast headquarters is located.

Each of these examples is indicative of Google's tendency to turn its own complexity into a source of advantage, and even highlights how Google IT can empower Google customers and not just the Googlers mentioned in the mission.

The mission statement's third implication is that Google IT's development methods will be agile, as Google's competitors are many and varied, and they are not treading water. Agile methods deliver projects and capabilities quicker, and speed to deliver is essential. On this front, Fried and his team have one of the best user acceptance testing groups immediately at hand in the form of Google employees in the surrounding cubes and offices. Again, this provides ample room for feedback, advice, and ongoing iterations of projects that more fully flesh out what is valuable and what is not.

Through its mission definition and related steps, Fried and his team have laid the foundation that has enabled the enviable growth and success of the company in the past half decade; and like the company itself, he and his team continue to think of ways to add more value to the company as a whole.[1]

Marriott IT: Vision, Mission, and Value Proposition

Marriott is one of many IT organizations that have both a vision and a mission. At Marriott, the vision is the more general statement, and the mission provides an additional level of specificity regarding the plans that they maintain. I find their example of special interest because it granulates one level even further than their overarching vision and mission statements, making crystal clear to employees within IT, as well as for those who partner with IT internally and externally, how IT means to direct behavior and ultimately the culture of the organization.

Bruce Hoffmeister, the global CIO of Marriott, developed a set of ideas he titled "Powering Marriott Through Technology." To that, he linked the following vision:

> We are innovative business leaders powering
> competitive advantage for Marriott and our brands,
> who anticipate technology trends and adapt to emerg-
> ing opportunities while delivering core functions
> flawlessly.

Vision and Value

At many points, the phrasing and layers to this vision highlight a new kind of IT value proposition.

"Innovative business leaders . . ." The first descriptor is that the IT department is to be a group of innovative business leaders. The focus on business innovation is relatively new for IT departments, and calling out IT as a function made up of business leaders

is also still not the norm, unfortunately, as I mentioned a few pages back. This can be seen in the typical reference to IT versus the business: "IT and the business," as though they are separate entities. Hoffmeister suggests that they are one and the same—IT *is* the business.

"*. . . Powering competitive advantage for Marriott and our brands . . .*" IT also needs to be a source of competitive advantage for Marriott. This is again a very powerful statement, suggesting that IT is not just keeping the lights on, making sure that the telephones work, making sure that the email is up and running, but that it needs to be a source of competitive advantage. It needs to be a differentiator for the organization. In other words, IT should provide the sorts of capabilities that will drive consumers to prefer one's brand.

"*. . . Who anticipate technology trends and adapt to emerging opportunities . . .*" It also calls out the need to anticipate technology trends, and this is a theme that is already explored in the book but bears repeating. Technology needs to be an R&D function of sorts, constantly looking around the next corner to identify the next trend that is appropriate for the organization to leverage. Identifying the trends that will apply best to the company is obviously an important qualifier. Trends are only as good as their application and ultimate value creation for the company itself, and IT needs to act as a translator.

"*. . . While delivering core functions flawlessly.*" This last phrase is really the foundational point, but I like the fact that Hoffmeister calls it out last. "While delivering core functions flawlessly" gets back to the whole notion of IT's core job, which is making sure that the core systems, infrastructure, all of the technology components that IT is responsible for, need to be up, available, and doing what they're meant to do. Ken Venner, current CIO of SpaceX and former Broadcom CIO, calls it "like air, an assumption that we have, that it is going to be there."[2]

Hoffmeister makes the appropriate point that if IT is not delivering what it is supposed to be doing from an infrastructure perspective or from an applications perspective—if IT isn't up and available—then all else does not matter. Moreover, you are not going to be asked to be innovative. You're not going to be given the opportunity to be a source of competitive advantage. You're not going to be asked to spend time on new trends and new things. Ultimately, you are not likely to be the CIO for very long.[3]

Marriott IT's More Specific Mission

Hoffmeister goes on to define "Our Mission" (IT's mission) in terms of five components.

1. *"Anticipate technology trends and adapt to emerging opportunities."* This brings up the very important point that IT needs to be collaborative. IT needs to be, at its core, a networked part of the organization, identifying both internal and external strategic opportunities and partnerships. It's important to note that this is with colleagues as well as with external partners of various kinds in order to develop strategies that are in fact innovative.

2. *"Grow our industry leadership position with holistic solutions."* There are two interesting points to this: that there are going to be core platforms; that is, don't choose many different technologies, but when possible, actually limit the technology footprint to a core set that will be focal where investment will be made. Also, limit the number of additional components that may take away from that focus, and then use that as a source of differentiation for the organization.

3. *"Deliver innovative technology reliably, predictably, and cost-effectively."* If you cannot do the basics with a degree of certainty and professionalism, your colleagues will not trust you with funds to be more adventurous and innovative.

4. *"Enable people to use information for strategic decision making."* This calls out the aforementioned point that IT is often

responsible for the pipes but doesn't necessarily pay enough attention to what's flowing through them. The information that makes up half of the name of the information technology function needs to be focal. A key value proposition for the IT department of the future will be to empower colleagues to tap information for insight, which will yield value through more informed, timely decisions.

5. *"Create meaningful opportunities for IT professionals."* The IT department is only as good as the people who are a part of it, so it is important that IT, like other departments, invest in its people. Perhaps a key additional point is that the dynamism of IT requires that an ongoing investment be made in people, whether it's reinvigorating the organization's existing staff with training on new technology or augmenting the team's existing skills with the fresh perspectives and talents of new hires. These are the ways of ensuring that IT is up to date on the latest and greatest from a technology perspective and not falling behind. It is easy to go from high performance to average performance by not investing in people and in new skills that are anticipating the needs of the organization as it continues to evolve, and IT needs to be firmly cognizant of that imperative.

Marriott IT's Third Level: "How We Create Value"

Now a key differentiator, a level that I don't regularly see IT leaders taking in their vision and mission continuum, is defined by Hoffmeister as "How We Create Value." Here again, he makes five main points, and I was thrilled when I read that the number one point, literally IT's first word in "How We Serve," was "listen":

1. *"Listen to our partners to understand business opportunities."* IT departments and IT leaders historically have not been known as necessarily the best listeners, yet listening is the

first key ingredient to being a good partner. As IT is delivering the needs of the business, it needs to make sure that it also facilitates conversations that will define those needs as effectively as possible. That means asking very good questions (starting with ones such as Jo-ann Olsovsky asked in Chapter Two), then sitting back and listening, and summarizing the key points to demonstrate an understanding. Certainly this doesn't mean that it is a solely passive experience. IT needs to be a counselor and a consultant of sorts to the rest of the organization, pushing its thinking, suggesting the new or unthought of. It begins with listening.

2. *"Provide strategic insights to drive the right solution."* It is not surprising that Hoffmeister, an executive who grew up in the finance function at Marriott, would call out the need to think about the way in which IT *articulates its value proposition in business terms*. As Hoffmeister himself says, system uptime is merely "par for the course in many ways. It is the expectation. We need to define value in a better way, in terms that our colleagues understand." So, for instance, this means that everyone in IT must understand the key metrics of the business, such as revenue per available room ("revPAR" as the hoteliers say), a key metric in the hotel and hospitality space. As Hoffmeister says, if there is anyone in IT who does not understand the inner workings of the revPAR metric, that is problematic. So an important part of his own training for all employees is making sure they understand those key metrics and think further about IT's potential contribution to those metrics.

3. *"Be easy to work with; use clear processes and flexible thinking."* The process point is squarely within the bailiwick of IT departments in general, and process excellence ought to be the goal for leading IT departments. For IT to be as agile and flexible as possible, a key is to have *repeatable* processes.

Too many organizations do not have clear processes and as a result must redefine how they do things each time. Typically, things proceed in an ad hoc fashion, and valuable time is wasted. Having clear processes matters greatly, along with some flexibility to them.

4. *"Foster experimentation through trial and error, balancing risk with reward."* Part of what the flexible processes and the agility ought to bring about is the ability to try things, to fail fast, and to learn from those unsuccessful trials so that the subsequent trials are more successful and build off past experiments. This needs to be a key aspect to the IT protocol as well.

5. *"'See around the corner' and advance future technologies."* This implies IT's need to be cognizant of and engaged in the evolution of business in general, and technology more specifically, in order to apply emerging technologies in a compelling fashion that delivers value—in business terms—back to the organization.

This very comprehensive Marriott IT framework can be used for onboarding new IT employees, can be a filter for existing IT employees to determine priorities, and can be a cultural rallying point as to where IT ought to fit into the rest of the organization.

Common Factors in Other IT Missions

Figure 3.1 displays IT missions in use at various leading companies. Notice what these mission statements have in common:

- *Inclusive language:* All-inclusive language, such as "we" or the company name, establishes collective ownership and personal investment in the mission.
- *Proactive stance:* Many mission statements are proactive in nature, using language such as "drive," "actively contribute," "forward thinking," and so on.

Company	CIO	Mission Statement
Microsoft	Jim DuBois	"Microsoft IT connects the company, delights customers and inspires the industry."
McKesson	Randy Spratt	"McKesson IT will drive competitive advantage by enabling technology-based innovation and by delivering quality, cost-competitive services."
Procter & Gamble	Filippo Passerini	"To transform the way business is done."
San Francisco Giants	Bill Schlough	"We are dedicated to providing professional, responsive customer service while developing, implementing and supporting innovative IT solutions that enable the attainment of the Giants' strategic objectives."
BNSF	Jo-ann Olsovsky	"We partner with the business to understand core processes and leverage technology to improve BNSF efficiency and competitive advantage. We are forward thinkers and good stewards of the technology investments we deploy."
Global Partners LP	Ken Piddington	"Actively contribute to the success of the organization through quality service delivery and innovation."
Red Hat	Lee Congdon	"To be a service-driven information technology organization and a trusted business partner, delivering flexible, effective solutions to our customers."
Amtrak	Jason Molfetas	"We will be a world class team that proactively delivers cost effective, secure, and innovative business solutions."

Figure 3.1. Current IT Missions at a Variety of Leading Companies.

- *Innovation:* Three of the statements mention "innovation," revealing the need for technology to be constantly exploring new avenues of value, rather than just maintaining a back office.

- *Business success:* Almost all of the mission statements maintain a focus on the true end game, and place an emphasis on supporting or driving business success and "competitive advantage," not just IT success.

- *Partnership:* All of the statements use language such as "service," "enable," or "partner" to suggest that IT cannot and should not operate in a vacuum, but rather can be most effective when enhancing the value that other disciplines offer.

- *Customer centricity:* There is an allusion to or a direct mention of end customers in some of the statements, suggesting a need to create value through IT for the people who buy the company's products or services.

- *Action-oriented:* Most of the mission statements explicitly call out "delivery," suggesting that IT will not sit idly but will produce tangible value in various forms for the organization.

- *Accountability:* This theme runs through each of the statements. Accountability and transparency are qualities that IT needs to embrace, and even lead on, as it is essential that IT leadership encourage the rest of the organization to be accountable and transparent, as well.

Where a Mission Is Most Needed

Creating a value-oriented IT mission is particularly important in those scenarios in which the IT department does not have much guidance from the rest of the organization, does not yet have a strong IT strategy per se, or both. It is a great first point of orientation for the IT department. That said, it is also highly effective to continue to keep in place for the IT team in general to learn, almost like a mantra. This helps focus the entire team on those principles that are most important, and it provides guidance on behaviors to exhibit on a daily basis, including factors to look for when recruiting, criteria to use in evaluating internal talent, and additional factors to consider when contracting with an external partner or vendor.

In Chapter Four, we return to our main agenda of how to develop and flesh out a full IT strategy by first helping Corporate and other divisions develop strategies of their own.

IT Mission Take-Aways

1. Creating a mission statement is a fast way to begin to find "true north" and to distinguish meaningful projects from those that ought to be filtered out, especially when corporate and divisional objectives are being expressed as simplistic "targets." It is also a good first step toward developing a true IT strategy.

2. Projects should be the outcome of missions and strategies, not the drivers of them.

3. As you create a mission statement, think in terms of the value proposition of IT. Will the statement make it easy to see how IT is likely to contribute to overall financial value?

4. What does your mission statement need to say about IT as a developer of processes and other future assets versus its ongoing role in delivering core functions?

5. Be able to "deconstruct" your mission statement into highly meaningful and prescriptive phrases.

6. Use your mission statement as a starting point to coax other divisions toward clearer strategies.

7. Consider going further by describing how IT wants to behave (for example, "how to serve").

8. Articulate where in IT and its staff you can put your mission statement to immediate practical use as a guideline or filter:

   - In metrics
   - In recruitment
   - Elsewhere within IT

4

Facilitating Corporate
and Divisional Strategy

It may seem presumptuous to say that CIOs should push the heads of other divisions of the company to craft their strategies, and to do so in a new way, as this chapter will describe. The CIO's peers and superiors might chafe at the thought that IT would deign to suggest such a thing. The CIO is the executive who is most adversely affected by a lack of strategy in other divisions. Moreover, and more persuasively perhaps to the other executives, unless CIOs can get divisions to align on how they go about creating and expressing strategy, CIOs cannot take advantage of their valuable niche in the corporate structure, which spans across all divisions, to note opportunities for collaboration across the company and places where technology or better management of information can bring to life the opportunities articulated by multiple divisions.

CIOs must press the rest of the organization to develop plans using a common framework, even if the substance of those plans will be quite different, division by division. In this chapter, I will provide an overview of the process a CIO can use to make the case for and pursue this aim. As I said earlier, there's more than one model for strategy creation that can serve as a common framework, but here I will unify my discussion around OGTM (objectives, goals, tactics, measures), the strategy model I introduced in Chapter Two. I have intentionally not tied the fictional example here to a particular industry, as I hope that the somewhat generic process will be easy for you to translate to your own. In this fictional case, as happens often in reality, there is a mandate for change in our company, "Zircon." Let's get started.

An Executive Mandate, But . . .

The CEO of Zircon has just declared that this will be "The Year of the Customer." In his rationale, he notes that in recent years the company has focused on internal process improvement and on the development of new products and services, but has not done enough to focus on Zircon's external customers, understanding their needs, determining where they have been happy with the company and its products and service offerings and where they have not been. Zircon senior management has been worrying that competitors with closer ties to customers and more sophisticated marketing programs and sales techniques could threaten Zircon, even if Zircon offers better products and services. Fortunately, in addition to stating the customer-focus objective, the CEO has also specified a "SMART" (see Chapter Two) metric of success: "We aim to improve customer satisfaction rates, as evaluated by customer surveys, from 70 percent satisfied to 85 percent satisfied by the end of the next fiscal year."

As we shall see, the combination of a clearly stated objective and "SMART" success measure will serve three important purposes:

- It will help us to prioritize and plan resourcing of initiatives.
- It will provide a mandate for all functions to pursue and measure progress toward the objective.
- It will summarize a strategic goal and desired end state for internal and external stakeholders, potentially including partners, vendors, and investors.

Interpreting the Mandate

In many companies, the C-level executives (COO, CFO, CMO, and so on) and divisional as well as functional heads are left to translate the CEO's mandated objective, as they lead and operate within their respective departments. Sometimes they do so effectively, but all too often the resulting new divisional and functional plans remain opaque to other departments or divisions and, as a result, they remain disconnected. Disconnection undermines the overall organization's ability to focus resources and so leads to a loss of overall effectiveness. Disconnection and opacity may hinder the IT department even more than other cross-divisional units. Without clarity across the board, IT has no way to ensure that it devotes appropriate time and efforts to the real imperatives of the other divisions as they translate the overarching company objective ("customer focus") into divisional objectives. Suppose Marketing takes it to mean "develop customer-segmentation-based marketing campaigns"; Customer Service hears it as "develop Voice of the Customer feedback mechanisms"; Operations takes it as "refine sense-and-respond supply chain capabilities, especially for customer delivery and return of products"; and so forth. Reporting back to the company as a whole, each division needs to render its interpretation at an equal level or degree of clarity and granularity so that these plans are understood by people within the divisions, first and foremost, but also so that other divisions who will collaborate to drive these plans forward will also clearly understand. Once the appropriate clarity and granularity is incorporated, IT can operate and cross-leverage across divisional plans to a greater extent, thus maximizing synergies, sequencing efforts appropriately, and optimizing business value add.

It is important to note that the traditional divisional silos of the company are in some ways antiquated. Yes, it is appropriate to have people with like experiences, training, and expertise aligned in the same division of the company to drive forward the activities embodied by the discipline of that division. Marketing is filled with marketers, Sales is filled with salespeople, and IT is filled with technologists. In this day and age, however, companies need to think much more across disciplines. Marketing needs to partner with IT in order to parse through the data that will help them make better marketing decisions. Salespeople need IT to help develop and manage solutions about what is selling where and why to help inform future decisions. Marketing and Sales must partner together in order to share insights about customers both current and potential. If the plans of any one of these three divisions are crafted in a way that is inaccessible to the others, friction is added where it should be eliminated, and the pace of seizing opportunities will slow.

In my experience over nearly two decades of advising CIOs, when reasonable requirements of cross-divisional clarity go unmet, many IT leaders have not recognized that they have a right if not an obligation to speak up. This leads to IT-business misalignment and results in inefficiency. Fortunately, a growing number of CIOs have recognized their need to push colleagues to develop their plans in a better, clearer, and more cohesive fashion, highlighting that it is a benefit not only to IT but for the entire organization (and its stakeholders and customers), since clarity better equips each division of the company to understand the plans of the others. CIOs cannot succeed here without getting from the other executives true cooperation and appreciation of the idea of involving the technology function in strategic planning conversations and exercises. Even in organizations in which IT capabilities are mainly internally focused, willing cooperation is needed. The fact is that high-performance and industry-leading organizations proactively involve IT executives and make strategic planning a truly cross-functional exercise.

The CIO: Presumptuous or Logical?

Despite the preceding, in this discussion I'll stick with Zircon, where the situation is not optimal. Let's picture Zircon as a company where strategic planning is limited at best in its various divisions, and each feels isolated and defensive about the idea that IT would intrude to facilitate strategic conversations between them.

At Zircon, when the CIO begins to ask questions suggesting the need to clarify the plans of each of the divisions of the company, she sounds presumptuous to the division heads. Who is she to ask questions about their strategic plans? At Zircon the pattern has been for divisions to "place orders" with the IT department, engaging IT only when full technology solutions have been dreamed up; any early engagement seems pointless and unusual. Here it's up to the CIO to make the case for becoming involved. The advantage CIOs have in this is that logic is on their side. For example, Zircon's CIO embraces the CEO's mandate of customer focus and wants to support the divisions along the same lines. To that end, IT is developing ideas for the coming year on what to develop, and it wants to make sure those ideas match with the most important business needs and opportunities that each division has identified. To ensure a match, it needs to understand, at a strategic level, what each division intends.

Of course, the logic holds up only if the CIO sufficiently understands the company's business, is steeped in solid business frameworks, and has some idea of how to leverage one or more frameworks in meetings with divisional leaders, in the interest of mutual clarity. Among various tried-and-true frameworks, for instance, is Porter's Five Forces analysis, an environmental analysis and strategic planning method developed by Michael Porter of Harvard Business School, which addresses

- Threat of new entrants
- Threat of substitute products or services
- Bargaining power of customers (buyers)
- Bargaining power of suppliers
- Intensity of competitive rivalry[1]

Focus Not on IT

At Zircon (and elsewhere) these conversations between the IT and divisional leaders start out with the division heads and their leadership teams tending to talk about IT needs and the technology-related aspects of the needs of the division. This seems right to them, since it is IT that wanted to meet. However, the IT leader must respectfully push back and ask for the actual *business* needs rather than the subset of technology aspects or potential solutions.

The IT leader needs to suggest, for example, "Let *us* determine which of your needs can be addressed with IT-driven automation, and which cannot." A conversation that focuses on divisional heads dreaming up IT solutions will be limited—whether by technology understanding, feasibility, or otherwise—and it will not get to root causes of business or operational issues that the solutions are supposed to address. Moreover, the head of a division other than IT should not be as educated about what IT can do. That is IT's primary area of expertise and source of value to the company. Conversely, however, IT leaders today are expected to be intimately familiar with fundamental business issues so that potential IT solutions can be developed with that business-value creation or contribution in mind.

In my experience, these ongoing and often iterative business and IT conversations, which do not necessarily have to be limited to the senior-most leadership, produce tangible and sometimes even surprising results, such as an IT leader dismissing a technology-centric solution but at the same time offering alternative business practices.

IT and Marketing: An Example of Facilitation Using SWOT Analysis

IT's facilitation for Marketing can be a matter of work directly between IT and Marketing, but in addition you can involve an external advisor who does not have skin in the game and who may be able to provide more of an external perspective. Even then, however, the important thing is the collaboration between the leaders and experts of Marketing who produce the data for analysis and those of IT who help them synthesize it. This is a great service that IT provides, and one that is likely to burnish the credentials of IT leadership for undertaking this type of activity elsewhere in the company and on a continuous basis.

Let's consider an opening conversation between Zircon's CIO and CMO. The CIO might begin as follows:

> Our CEO says this needs to be "The Year of the Customer." Each of us needs to translate this to determine what we can do to have a positive impact on our customers' experience with our firm. As CMO, you're interpreting the customer focus objective in marketing terms. In IT, naturally our leadership team will need to think in terms of technology. To do our job well, the IT team will need to understand your translation of the objective. Once we understand that, we can insert ourselves with suggestions of where automation or other applications of technology can help you initiate and support your plans—as we hope to do for every division.

For reasons mentioned in Chapter Two, a good way to proceed from there involves a basic SWOT analysis (strengths, weaknesses, opportunities, and threats). SWOT analysis was originally developed by Albert Humphrey.[2] It aims at identifying strategic themes that have the potential to evolve into strategic objectives. Most likely you are already familiar with its definitions of the four legs of the analysis. The first two focus internally, on the division or company itself, in its present state:

Strengths. Areas of accomplishment or sources of advantage for the company or division in question

Weaknesses. Areas of disadvantage or not-as-yet-addressed gaps in the company or division in question

The third and fourth look externally and toward the future:

Opportunities. A favorable juncture of circumstances that the company or division may wish to exploit

Threats. Something that could cause future trouble or harm to the company or division

In the discussion between the CIO and CMO and their teams, each party performs the analysis as it appears to them, from their respective vantage points, in relation to their common agenda—in this case, "The Year of the Customer."

Marketing's SWOT

As feedback during the SWOT discussion at Zircon, let's suppose the CMO and his Marketing leaders appraise themselves as shown in Figure 4.1.

The figure illustrates what's happening with a much shorter list of items and observations than is typical of most SWOT analyses. In practice, SWOT analyses may have many tens or even hundreds of SWOT data or observations. In those cases, for the sake of refinement and clarity, it is essential to categorize and label SWOT data according to types, such as those listed in Figure 4.2. The list we show is by no means exhaustive, rather a starting point for any SWOT process as it adds structure to the analysis. Naturally, the Zircon CIO and CMO would specify a set of types that best fits Marketing's, Zircon's, or the industry's needs.

Next, it is useful to develop a simple statistical analysis to determine which of the SWOT data types are most relevant in an organization's current-state analysis—one simple yet unscientific approach is to assess which ones are most commonly referred to by employees in the different functional areas that are involved in

Type	Strengths	Weaknesses	Opportunities	Threats	Total
Customers		• We do not gather comprehensive data on our customers. • We do not have enough information from our customers to truly understand what they want or need.	• We could develop an incentive for our customers to provide more information to us so that we can provide products or services that more specifically meet their needs. • We could develop more sophisticated customer relationship management (CRM) methods and solutions to determine more definitively who our best customers are and who our best potential customers are.		4
People	• We have some of the most talented marketing employees in the industry. • We have deep ties to marketing departments at leading business schools, which we can tap for research and for talent.	• Our younger staff tend not to stay with the company for a long time.		• If more of our Marketing staff leave, significant marketing knowledge will leave with them that we will not be able to replicate.	4

Figure 4.4. A Digest of SWOT Observations Gathered by Marketing at Zircon.

Type	Strengths	Weaknesses	Opportunities	Threats	Total
Technology		• We do not have strong technical know-how in Marketing. • Our customer databases are antiquated and do not facilitate efficient and effective decision making.			2
Competition				• More nimble companies may market their flexibility as key differentiators compared to us. • Our investments in our company (which outpaced our investments in our customers) render us vulnerable to being outmarketed by our competition.	2
Geography or Market			• We could obtain and leverage better demographic data to understand which geographies to enter or emphasize.		1
Total	2	5	3	3	13

Figure 4.4. A Digest of SWOT Observations Gathered by Marketing at Zircon. (*Continued*)

be more creative in developing products and services that more squarely meet their needs. Marketing also sees a need for better customer relationship management processes and tools in order to collect and leverage data to make better marketing decisions. This suggests two needs:

- To develop the capabilities to more effectively market to the company's best customers
- To upgrade processes and technology to make Marketing efforts more efficient and effective

In addition, the organization has great people and a source for new blood through the relationships with business schools. The new hires into Marketing tend to be fickle, and there is a worry that when they leave, they leave with a tremendous amount of knowledge. This suggests more needs:

- To create incentives for the best staff to remain in the Marketing department and the company longer
- To invest in better knowledge management processes and solutions in order to document the most important information to be passed from employees who depart to new employees

The two weaknesses related to technology in Figure 4.4 suggest another need:

- To upgrade technical skills and solutions in Marketing to be the best in the industry

From SWOT to OGTM

Once the SWOT is complete, the inputs for the creation of the strategic planning framework (the OGTM) are in place.

Objectives for Marketing

Any of the needs determined in the preceding section could be starting points for strategic objectives for the Marketing department. In fact, collectively, these could be the objectives for the department for the foreseeable future (a realistic strategic planning horizon of three to five years, for example), and there would be solid SWOT data to back them up. As an example, let's make the first of the needs a strategic objective for Marketing. A strategic OGTM framework addressing that objective might look something like Figure 4.5. Notice how, at this stage, the form expands from what you saw in Figure 2.6, with multiple tactics and measures.

Note that the tactics that are listed in the OGTM are not necessarily IT-centric even though IT may well have helped draft this document on the basis of inputs from colleagues in Marketing. It is important to note those actions that the Marketing department can take, whether alone or in conjunction with partners in other functional areas, in order to accomplish what is suggested by the objective and goal.

Later, in concert with other planning that is going on outside Marketing (and between it and IT, Corporate, and other divisions) Marketing will be equipped to expand its OGTM documents with details about how individual tactics will be carried out and by whom, and how measures will be obtained. You will see this unfold in Chapter Six, where we work through the development of IT's OGTM, which, optimally, should come after the corporate and other divisional OGTMs have been finalized. Mind you, the CIO may not have this luxury, and if he or she does not have the buy-in from divisional leaders to develop their OGTMs, the CIO may need to develop the IT OGTM first using inputs from strategic conversations with other leaders.

Commonalities with Other Divisions

Of course, Marketing is just one of several divisions that should play a significant role in "The Year of the Customer," and optimally,

Marketing Objective	Goals (Objective KPIs)
Develop the capabilities to more effectively market to the company's best customers	Improve profitability per customer by 10 percent by the end of the next fiscal year

Tactics	Measures (Tactic KPIs)
Develop a better means of collecting and sorting customer data	Decrease the time it takes to refresh Marketing campaigns from three weeks to one week by the end of the next fiscal year
Define the qualities that make up the best customers	Increase the percentage of Marketing's budget spent targeting the best customers by the end of next fiscal year
Determine what sorts of products and services the best customers typically buy from the company and connect the dots between best customers and the favored products or services	Increase revenue generated from these favored products and services by 25 percent by the end of the next fiscal year
Provide opportunities for the IT department and the Marketing department to cross-pollinate resources	Identify three new Marketing campaigns developed by cross-functional IT and Marketing resources by the end of the fiscal year
Develop predictive ability to determine who among potential customers are likely to be future "best customers"	Increase the percentage of new customers acquired who are in the "best customer" category to 50 percent of all new customers within two years

Figure 4.5. Expanding One Marketing Objective.

IT will have been a part of the other divisions' SWOT and OGTM planning as well. For example, at Zircon, the process in the Sales division might lead to an objective for Sales of "increasing the effectiveness of sales efforts." Figure 4.6 shows some beginning OGTM for that Sales objective.

Sales Objective	Goals (Objective KPIs)
Increase the effectiveness of sales efforts	Increase sales yield by 35 percent within two years
Tactics	**Measures (Tactic KPIs)**
Develop tools to track customer data	Decrease the time it takes to develop proposals from an average of one week to an average of one day by the end of the fiscal year
Develop a better sales commission process that provides incentives to bring in multiple business disciplines for each sales call	Decrease the number of meetings required to close on each sale from four to two by the end of the next fiscal year
Develop better product and service bundles, targeting the best customers	Increase the percentage of sales that include at least two products or services to 50 percent of total sales within two years
Provide opportunities for the IT division and the Sales division to cross-pollinate resources	Sell 20 percent more products and services within two years to five targeted IT-centric customers with resources who have been cross-pollinated
Track sales call data in real time	Decrease the number of people required to answer RFPs from five to two within two years

Figure 4.6. An Objective in Zircon Sales.

The Larger Cascade

You can begin to see some commonalities between the sample OGTM from Marketing and the one from Sales. Read through the tactics, especially for similar intentions. As we will do in Chapter Five, a CIO and his or her leadership team can mine details from Marketing and Sales OGTMs (especially at the levels of tactics and measures) for their own internal planning purposes and the development of the IT OGTM. With this in mind, flip back briefly to Figure 2.7.

Figure 2.7 also shows how the OGTMs at the divisional level should connect to the OGTM at the corporate level, the objectives and goals at the divisional level becoming the tactics and measures at the corporate level. In Chapter Two, I referred to this connection of different strategic frameworks between the divisional and corporate levels as a critically important "strategic cascade." This is

Zircon Objective	Goals (Objective KPIs)
Make the next fiscal year "The Year of the Customer"	Improve customer satisfaction rates as evaluated by customer surveys from 70 percent satisfied to 85 percent satisfied by the end of the next fiscal year
Tactics	**Measures (Tactic KPIs)**
Develop the capabilities to more effectively market to the company's best customers	Improve profitability per customer by 10 percent by the end of the next fiscal year
Increase the effectiveness of sales efforts	Increase sales yield by 35 percent within two years
(. . .)	(. . .)

Figure 4.7. The Corporate OGTM, Building on Objectives That Came Up from Marketing and Sales.

a cascade with a twist, in that strategy cascades *down* (for example, from C-level to lower, mid-level managers) and *up* (from divisional, functional, and geographic leaders to the corporate strategists).

Figure 4.7 provides a graphical representation of how the two objectives and their respective goals shown in the Marketing OGTM Figure 4.5 and the Sales OGTM Figure 4.6 might "cascade up" to appear among the tactics and measures for Zircon's corporate-level grand objective, "Make the Next Fiscal Year the Year of the Customer."

Together, the figures begin to show everyone at Zircon how the OGTM process that IT initiated with several divisions enhances its value as it grows, and with it the value of IT.

A Real-World Example: Red Robin

Chapter Two gave you the real-world example of Jo-ann Olsovsky, a CIO who was bold enough to undertake an exercise like the one I've just described using the fictional company Zircon. To highlight how this is done, I would like to provide a second real-world example, this time from a CIO from a very different industry: restaurants.

Ten years ago, the thought of a CIO leading strategy for the company would have seemed preposterous. Indeed there are many companies today for which it still seems so. I submit that this resistance has more to do with individuals who occupy the CIO position than with the role of the CIO in general. In a time when businesses are doing more through better use of technology, partly driven by the nature of an organization's core business activities but also driven by changes across all industries, the CIO role requires intimate conversations with every leader of the company on a regular basis. Digital channels and digital businesses are becoming the norm, even in businesses that were previously considered classic "brick and mortar" operations. Many of the predominant business trends require at least some new IT components, and many cannot happen at all without them. A particularly clever CIO should recognize the powerful perch on which he or she has been placed and take off from it to be part of the conversations in which strategy is set.

The example that follows goes into the details of the business circumstance the CIO found upon arriving at the company. Just as I have emphasized throughout, the business inputs are essential precursors to the development of IT strategy, and the CIO who facilitates this kind of conversation will earn tremendous credibility with other executives, perhaps even being asked to lead strategy for the company.

Disconnection's Inflection

In June of 2007, Chris Laping became CIO of Red Robin Gourmet Burgers, a publicly traded restaurant organization based near Denver, Colorado. When he arrived, he found an IT team searching for purpose, its work disconnected from the plans of the organization as a whole. Somehow strategy was not translating appropriately into day-to-day IT activities.

Laping used skills he had acquired previously as a consultant and as a CIO to get to the root of the problem. It wasn't obvious right away, because the company had enjoyed enormous success and growth since its inception in 1969, and who should question success? As he delved into the details, however, he found that IT was not the only department acting independently. Across the organization there was no integrated and organized strategic plan. What strategy existed was not universally getting passed, translated, and filtered through the divisions of the company, so that there was a limited line of sight between the activities of each division and the broader objectives of the organization. Each division had its own plans but was operating largely in a silo, disconnected and without the sharing across divisions of common objectives and measurement. As a result, as IT interacted with each division, drawing out thoughts on needs and translating those into IT projects, each division leader had little idea about what other division leaders were demanding of IT. Laping recognized that the problem of this disconnection would only get worse as the company grew. When he joined Red Robin in 2007, the organization was on the path to reaching $1 billion in revenues within a few years (they did so in 2013). As it happens, I have found that revenue threshold tends to be an inflection point at which a lack of a clear strategy becomes a significant hindrance.

Laping's Response

Rather than choosing a radical reengineering process, which might have failed before it proved its value, Laping developed a series of steps to reach his ultimate destination.

Developing a Cross-Divisional Forum

As part of the first step, Laping began by creating a technology prioritization team (TPT). This was the first forum that brought together leaders from across Red Robin to hear from each other about needs, wants, and demands of IT, and to hear what IT proposed to do in order to address those needs, wants, and demands. In the past, IT had had to prioritize IT projects itself, and, naturally, some divisional leaders had been upset when they had found that their top priorities were not being pursued, or that these would only be tackled after other projects were implemented. In initial meetings of the TPT, leaders from outside of IT finally got a clearer picture of how their demands might compare with peers' demands. This TPT process was so successful that Laping was asked to apply the process to all projects, not just IT projects. This was just the opening he needed to weave himself more tightly into the strategy-setting process for the entire company.

Developing a Vision

Around this time, Steve Carley joined the company as CEO. Before his arrival, the vision for the company as a whole had been "to be the most respected restaurant company in terms of how we treat our team members, guests, and shareholders—in that order." In Carley's estimation, this vision was too corporate and internally focused, with far too little attention focused on the guest. He also questioned whether the vision was clear enough to drive action. He saw the need to develop a new vision centered on the guest's perspective. The shift was subtle in some ways but had substantial consequences, as it focused the organization on enhancing the guest experience. Happy guests translate into loyal customers who will return to Red Robin more frequently. From there, the vision statement evolved into something simpler that enabled team members to connect their activities with what guests were looking for. In fact, the vision took the form of words from the customer's mouth:

> I crave Red Robin's burgers so much it's my "go-to" place for burgers and fries unless I absolutely have no time to dine in. No matter who I am with or what I am looking for, I am always so delighted with the service and my experience, I want to tell my friends.

Embracing this vision, Laping jumped right in to address the broader strategic questions of what the company wanted to represent and how it could do so. With the customer vision statement in mind, Laping and the rest of the company's executive team dug into the details of Red Robin's guest feedback and other consumer insight.

In a few areas the company scored high: the restaurant was a fun place for families to eat together, the brand was clearly differentiated by consumers, and it had strong brand recognition and consideration. However, in a number of areas guests told Red Robin it could improve. One was the lack of a particular menu item that they craved. The company was known for great hamburgers, but no one burger stood out as the one that people craved. Red Robin's leaders also discovered that the restaurant was not as comfortable a place to dine for adults without children. The last thing that adult friends want is to go out to dinner and be seated next to screaming kids. Also, a number of customers indicated that the restaurant was not as affordable as it should be. The average cost of a hamburger was $9 to $10 all told, and several customers who were polled noted that this was not a price point that would enable them to return frequently to Red Robin.

Laping's Key Addressable Items

Laping analyzed this customer feedback and pressed to develop a short list of "key addressable items" (KAIs) to tackle the issues. He wanted the nature of each item to be clear and accessible, expressed in plain language. He wanted each to be crisply defined, so that employees would not have to memorize sentences or phrases in order to develop ideas that connected with the issue. They also should be few in number, since one of Laping's goals was to develop an effective strategy in order to focus the organization. He came up with three key addressable items:

> *Cravability* was meant to address the need to create menu items that guests craved, together with techniques that would make that feasible.
>
> *Comfortability* was intended to help guests from across a wide spectrum of profiles, whether they gathered as families, as groups of adults, or as individuals, so that there was something to appeal to everyone.
>
> *Affordability* meant finding ways to lower costs to customers without eroding profits to the company.

These KAIs framed the strategy and initiatives that Laping's executive peers were collaboratively designing to transform the brand. They became the pillars of the new corporate strategic plan and the company's vision for an evolving strategy.

IT had a big role to play in all of these initiatives, especially in rendering the operation more efficient so that a portion of those efficiencies could be reflected back into the prices on the menu. Another opportunity was found in the notion of pricing bundles differently. Research had shown that although a $9 hamburger sounded expensive to diners, a meal consisting of a burger, a shake, and a dessert for $16 seemed reasonable to them. So a priority was set to draw further insights that would allow Red Robin to make its bundles more affordable and compelling.

The three addressable items, originally identified as a result of the CEO's desire to review and update the company's vision, led also to other objectives, goals, and addressable items for other aspects of the organization. Thus, in Red Robin's relationship with shareholders, objectives were defined as engagement, efficiency, and expansion. Each objective carries its own agenda of innovation and change that focuses on transforming people, place, and product at Red Robin.

Corporate-Wide IT

As Red Robin's overall agenda has taken shape, the company has enjoyed consistent and sustainable growth and accolades by industry analysts for its management team's effectiveness. Laping and his team were so successful that they now facilitate the strategy process for Red Robin as a whole, from what started as an IT-only perch. It is unusual for a CIO to do so, but why should it be? IT leaders need strategic clarity from the rest of the organization in order to suggest what IT can do to bring each plan to life. IT leaders also need strategic clarity to facilitate conversations about priorities.

One of the things I like best about Laping's story is that he was proactive. It bears repeating that many IT leaders who find themselves in situations in which plans are not conveyed with uniform clarity and granularity simply take this for granted, not wanting to offend anyone by suggesting that strategic planning must happen in a different way. Those leaders do not realize that they are walking into their own worst-case scenario: their company's success is perhaps leading to revenue growth, leading to more money to spend, but in turn leading to more uncontrolled, unprioritized demand on IT. More to do without a better way to manage that increased demand will only exacerbate their problems.

From OGTMs to Communication and Business Case

Laping makes the point that connecting the dots between the plans of the company and the activities of the individual is an ongoing process that needs continuous improvement. There was a point in early 2013 when the head of the IT program management office (PMO) left the company unexpectedly. As Laping did not have an immediate successor in mind, he elected to use the departure as an opportunity to dig deeper into the PMO's governance function, personally taking over responsibility for it as he searched for a new PMO leader. For part of a day each week, he held office hours in his old direct report's office. People were not allowed to schedule time with him during that stretch; if they wished to see him, they had to simply stop by.

Through the resulting interactions with various members of the PMO, he discovered that some of them did not see the connection between his plans, the company's plans, and what they did on a day-to-day basis. His first inclination was to think that the departed head of the PMO was at fault, "but I quickly came to the conclusion that this was *my* issue. I had not done well enough at this translation universally across the team, and I needed to think about creating more clarity and touch points."[3]

Part of the answer is smarter communications. Laping says that too often communications strategies resemble conversations with foreigners who do not speak our language. If the person with whom we are talking does not understand, we simply express ourselves louder instead of getting to the root cause of the breakdown. To maintain a regular and updated dialogue between himself and others, Laping says, "The key is to connect people with purpose. If people do not understand how they fit into the bigger picture, they will not have a purpose. Without a purpose, it is difficult to keep people motivated."

Laping also developed a mandate that any material effort requiring the time of members of his team would require a business case. First and foremost, there must be a line of sight between the proposed project and the objectives of the organization. Second, there must be a return on investment (ROI) assessment done on the activity. The project must track back to an objective. If it does not have an ROI, then questions are asked about the qualitative benefits of the project. If none can be identified, again, IT rejects the project. When a project makes it through these and other hurdles, then the people who are responsible for the project will understand the reason why they are working on it. In other words, they will have a sense of purpose.

Again, these practices have been adopted more broadly by the organization.

IT as Partner

Chris Laping's big three points of advice for CIOs who hope to follow in his footsteps are to be proactive, to be curious and exhibit that curiosity with one's colleagues, and to think of oneself as an advisor to the rest of the organization.

For a long time now, when I have spoken to CIOs (no matter the thrust of the presentation) I have tried to include in my message that CIOs need to stop using subservient language in their daily lives. There is no better example of this than to call one's colleagues "customers." If you think of your colleagues as customers, then there are the aforementioned three negative ramifications to this that I repeat here for emphasis:

1. You are declaring that you are less important than your colleagues, since customers are so clearly important to a company.
2. In the balance, the customer is always right, as the mantra goes, so defining colleagues as customers reduces your ability

to challenge your colleagues, even if the topic is in the domain
of information technology—where you are the master.

3. You distance yourself from the real and only customer: the end
customer who provides your business with its revenue.

These are profound consequences that seal the fate of IT as a support organization rather than a truly strategic one.

I have long said that one should refer to one's colleagues as
partners, suggesting parity and the need to collaborate. Laping
says that his preferred nomenclature is "advisor" to the rest of
the organization. He says, "Like a doctor, my team and I have an
area of expertise that is not the expertise of the rest of the organization. They should want my advice like we want the advice
from our doctors when our needs are in their areas of expertise."
Just as we are inclined to seek the counsel of doctors when we
are ill, for instance, and we are inclined to trust their diagnoses
and take the medicine that is suggested to us, IT should create as
essential a relationship with the rest of the organization, in which
IT's advice is sought and taken into account before decisions
are finalized.

In February 2011 Laping added the title of senior vice president
of Business Transformation to his CIO role. As the title suggests,
the SVP role is centered on innovation across the business. The
mission for the Business Transformation team is to drive and enable
change at Red Robin. It is understood that the success and failure of the brand rests squarely on the shoulders of its employees,
especially those within the restaurant, so there must be focus on
supporting them through change. Business Transformation builds
unique approaches for all key change initiatives (technical and
nontechnical) to ensure they are adopted successfully and in a stan-
dardized way, utilizing its five groups—Learning and Development,
Operations Services, Program Management, Product Management,
and IT. This provides a holistic approach to people, process, and
technology.

Ambition to Grow Further

It will not come as a surprise that Laping has ambition to become a CEO. Like the good strategist that he has proven himself to be, he is beginning with where he hopes to go, plotting his destination and then determining the steps to get there.

Through examples in this chapter we see how IT can and should take part in the creation of division-level OGTMs, and should help them connect what they do to the level of corporate objectives, where IT is also active. This brings us to the point at which we can get more deeply into how IT develops its own strategy, bearing in mind in equal parts the corporate and divisional strategies.

Facilitation Take-Aways

1. Proactively take a lead in pursuit of a company vision.
2. From your CIO perch with its broad view, press the rest of the organization to develop plans using a common framework, even though substance will differ across divisions.
3. Through using a common planning process, steer divisions to plan using language at comparable levels of clarity and granularity.
4. Steep yourself in solid business frameworks such as Porter's Five Forces analysis, and how to use them in conversation with colleagues from other divisions.
5. Facilitate strategy conversations with divisions, focusing not on IT but on a division's SWOT (or similar structured analysis). Help them reach a starting list of SWOTs.
6. Help each division study large numbers of comments and data related to each division and group them into types (areas of concern, such as "people," "processes," "technology," and so forth).
   - Develop a sortable database for use when SWOT data sets are large.

- Tabulate and study results in terms of which SWOTs and which types received either much or little attention.
- Draw some initial insights. Refine insights by digging deeper into the reliability and significance of particular comments and points of data. Use this process also to see how the typology can be refined and where data is thin and more should be gathered.
- Distill SWOT results down to few enough types and conclusions that they help you focus on a division's main priorities.
- After some refinement, look for connections across observations that fall in different SWOT types or categories. Use SWOT results to create division objectives to use in a strategy-planning framework such as OGTM (objectives, goals, tactics, measures).

7. Meanwhile, work with other divisions as well.
   - Use the unique perspective you gain to find commonalities that various divisions ought to take into account.
   - Help divisions coordinate their OGTMs with those of allied divisions.

8. Strengthen the strategic cascade.
   - Convey what you learn about division objectives and goals back up to Corporate to ensure alignment between divisions and the corporate-wide objective.
   - Work toward clearer understanding and coordination of aims at every level of IT and the company.

9. Move divisions toward making actual business cases and ROI analyses for projects they request from IT.

10. Partner with colleagues and other divisions, rather than treat them as customers (who "are always right").

11. Don't necessarily stop your own career thinking at the boundaries of IT.

5

IT Strategy Creation

Earlier chapters make it clear that IT strategy does not operate in a vacuum, but must take into consideration the strategies of the rest of the organization. Thus a new CIO or a CIO leading an immature IT department hoping to articulate a new strategy should engage the rest of the organization first for their plans before formulating one for IT.

As an IT department and the company around it mature in their ability to plan and to articulate strategic plans, the order becomes less important; insightful conversations can happen on a regular basis as dialogue flows freely in both directions. In that scenario it is still important to document corporate, divisional, and IT strategies, as it gives both junior and senior individuals insights into what will be focal for the year ahead, and what will not be focal, being absent from the plan. It also lets even the most junior staff see how their work ties into the highest-level strategy through the cascade.

The Listening CIO

A new CIO, even one promoted to that position from within, needs to listen before developing his or her own plans. Let me provide an example of a CIO who was promoted from within and proceeded to go on a listening tour of sorts before generating her plans. Here is the brief story of Kim Stevenson's first few months as the CIO of Intel.

Intel: Expecting Enough Value?

Kim Stevenson has one of the biggest jobs in information technology. As CIO of Intel, she leads a diverse team of technologists within a company that is historically known as a paragon of technology innovation. When she took her current post, she had been part of the IT leadership team already as a direct report to her predecessor. Yet, as a new CIO, she needed to develop a new relationship with her peers among the division heads and the broader Intel leadership team.

Speaking with other Intel leaders, Stevenson came to a surprising conclusion:

> The curious thing that I found was that our partners across the business were very satisfied with IT. As I dug deeper into the details, however, I discovered that they were using the wrong criteria to judge us. Many of my colleagues believed that Intel IT's highest calling was to develop programs and to foster service delivery. This is important for any IT department, but it is merely foundational. Believe it or not, I actually went back to my peers and superiors and said, "You are not expecting enough of IT."[1]

More specifically, other leaders had low or moderate expectations as to the innovation capabilities of IT, or didn't even consider IT as a natural source of innovation. Stevenson understood that if Intel was going to succeed in increasing its pace of innovation, IT needed to be more of a contributor to that innovation:

> Some of the folks I spoke with were flabbergasted. I explained that I want to directly contribute to business value and ultimately transform our business. Since then, I have led several initiatives aimed at raising expectations. This is the really interesting stuff, frankly, and it has been a wonderful way to motivate my team.

Kim Stevenson hasn't been the only head of an IT department to make this discovery. In my experience, I've worked with other IT leaders who have encountered low expectations of IT on the part of the other business leaders in their organization in terms of both innovation and business-value contribution. However, in one of the world's leading technology companies, that seems rather curious. In the case of Intel, Stevenson realized that to contribute more business value, her team needed to better understand the strategy of the rest of the organization. As they delved into what, according to Intel's strategy, was most important to the business units, she uncovered a variety of places where IT could make a difference and have a direct impact on the company's strategy:

> One of our big strategic imperatives is to accelerate development of systems on chips, which we refer to as SOCs. These are highly integrated chips that enable phones and tablets to be smaller in size, have a longer battery life, and have more capabilities, representing an evolution beyond Intel's traditional PC-centric micro-processors. Recognizing the importance and the critical role that IT could play, I focused IT's efforts to get more deeply involved supporting the next-generation SOCs.

Delving deeper into the strategic imperatives of the business, Stevenson realized that several of IT's existing strategic pillars remained valid. These included cloud, consumerization of IT, security, and business intelligence. As her team began to do some research into business and technology trends whose full values the company was not capturing, she saw two areas in need of further strategic focus and investment: social media and collaboration.

Stevenson also recognized a virtuous cycle she could create by establishing more strategic dialogue with her colleagues in Intel's business units:

> My peers and colleagues outside of IT were always avail-able for me to check in with, to test my theories, and to

seek their counsel. Thankfully, they never lack opinions, and they are generous in sharing ideas and insights. I was fortunate that my colleagues were quite engaged throughout. The more value we delivered as an IT department, the more inclined my colleagues outside of IT have been to engage us. This has been a powerful paradigm shift.

Exploring Cross-Functional Tactical Needs

While some of the material ahead focuses on other divisions, keep in mind that we are working toward clarifying IT's own strategy. The fastest path to doing so is to have members of the IT leadership team work with the rest of the divisions of the company as each is formulating plans. The path to a clear, concise, actionable, and valuable IT strategy lies in IT executives' ability to translate the needs of the various other divisions of the organization.

The first step in so doing is for a CIO to get to know the other leaders and their plans and needs so well that a shorthand develops between the CIO and those other leaders. The CIO gains the insights and eventually the trust of the other division executives to push their thinking, to disagree with them, to present alternatives, and the like. For a midsized or large company, the CIO probably cannot do this alone because as companies grow larger, the chances that they will have multiple business units, multiple geographies, or a greater variety of products and services will make it difficult for the CIO to remain abreast of everything on a week-to-week basis. In that case, being intimately involved in the business unit's operations becomes the job of a business information officer, or BIO.

Business Information Officers

Many companies have created the business information officer (BIO) role to create an easier method of harnessing strategic insights. Some companies refer to the role as business technology officer (BTO) or business relationship manager (BRM), to name just two of a variety of permutations that amount to similar roles. I like BIO because it is connected to the title of the CIO but emphasizes the fact that this is a business-centric role, reinforcing the fact that IT means business.

BIOs typically report to the CIO, but they often have a dotted-line reporting relationship with the head of another division of the company—the part of the company about which they will develop intimate knowledge. In fact, many times, the people who fill these roles are tech-savvy members of those very divisions, which is a wonderful way to bring IT and those divisions much closer, and to do so with a known commodity to the other division who clearly understands the nature of that division intimately. Optimally, the alignment is with a single division, though some IT departments align single individuals to multiple divisions. This may make sense for midsized or smaller companies in which there are limited resources in IT, but it tends not to be a tenable option for the behemoths, as the needs and topics are too varied for any one person to gain the level of depth of knowledge necessary to speak as a peer to the executives of the other divisions.

The BIO should be an advocate between IT and the other division, with an intimate knowledge of the strategy, plans, needs, opportunities, and issues of the division to which he or she is aligned but equal knowledge of IT's capabilities, skills, and strategy, so as to know what IT can deliver and when, and even suggest when an external partner may be the better option to partner with in order to deliver what is needed in a more timely, more cost-effective, or otherwise better fashion.

The BIO should attend all staff meetings with the CIO and with the leaders of the other division with which he or she is aligned. He or she should be present when each new idea is explained and act as an advisor and consultant.

Another distinct advantage of the BIO role is the opportunity for cross-BIO collaboration. This stimulates cross-divisional ideas, as often an idea generated for one division may apply to another one, but the lack of a forum to raise the possibility means that a higher percentage of the portfolio will be focused more on one-off ideas than should be the case. BIOs become an essential part of allowing IT to be strategic facilitators for the company while applying "glue" to more solidly bring the company closer together.

In the next chapter, we will cover some of the high-level insights regarding the role that enterprise architecture, or EA, plays in strategic planning, but I will briefly mention here that BIOs must develop a close tie with EA in order to understand how new opportunities and the projects that might bring them to life will work within the existing architecture, and the EA team may have new perspectives to provide that will suggest when existing architecture can be leveraged versus those cases in which the truly new must be introduced.

Searching for IT Strategic Insights in Divisional OGTMs

Now let's explore how CIOs, BIOs, and the other IT executives might mine divisional plans for insights, both on what can be delivered for those divisions and on the identification of common needs and ultimately the implications for IT's own plans. In Chapter Four, we saw how CIOs and their IT teams can work with divisional leadership to define strategic plans using the objectives, goals, tactics, and measures (OGTM) strategic framework. In the main example, the leadership team did so by deriving the inputs that Marketing provided and assembling plans at a level of clarity and granularity that was comparable across divisions. We noted that while some divisional heads may think IT presumptuous to insert itself in such an exercise, the examples of Jo-ann Olsovsky of BNSF Railway and Chris Laping of Red Robin Gourmet Burgers show that there are great rewards for technology leaders in getting more involved in strategic planning, including better prioritization, better demand management, higher-value IT investments, and potentially better work-life balance for staff.

One of the biggest values that IT can offer to the divisions in return for its being involved in planning to a greater degree than before is that IT can suggest areas where comparable needs appear across multiple plans. As an example, let's look at the strategic OGTM frameworks for Marketing and Sales introduced in the previous chapter side by side, as shown in Figure 5.1.

Marketing Objective	Goals (Objective KPIs)
Develop the capabilities to more effectively market to the company's best customers	Improve profitability per customer by 10 percent by the end of the next fiscal year
Tactics	**Measures (Tactic KPIs)**
(1) Develop a better means of collecting and sorting customer data	(1) Decrease the time it takes to refresh Marketing campaigns from three weeks to one week by the end of the next fiscal year
Define the qualities that make up the best customers	Increase the percentage of Marketing's budget spent targeting the best customers by the end of the next fiscal year
(2) Determine what sorts of products and services the best customers typically buy from the company and connect the dots between best customers and the favored product or service	(2) Increase revenue generated from these favored products and services by 25 percent by the end of the fiscal year
(3) Provide opportunities for the IT department and the Marketing department to cross-pollinate resources	(3) Identify three new Marketing campaigns developed by cross-functional IT and Marketing resources by the end of the fiscal year

Figure 5.1. Common Tactical Needs Identified Across Marketing and Sales.

Marketing Objective	Goals (Objective KPIs)
Develop predictive ability to determine who among potential customers are likely to be future "best customers"	Increase the percentage of new customers acquired who are in the "best customer" category to 50 percent of all new customers within two years

Sales Objective	Goals (Objective KPIs)
Increase the effectiveness of sales efforts	Increase sales yield by 35 percent within two years

Tactics	Measures (Tactic KPIs)
(1) Develop tools to track customer data	(1) Decrease the time it takes to develop proposals from an average of one week to an average of one day by the end of the fiscal year
Develop a better sales commission process that provides incentives to bring in multiple business disciplines for each sales call	Decrease the number of meetings required to close on each sale from four to two by the end of the next fiscal year
(2) Develop better product and service bundles, targeting the best customers	(2) Increase the percentage of sales that include at least two products or services to 50 percent of total sales within two years
(3) Provide opportunities for IT division and Sales division to cross-pollinate resources	(3) Sell 20 percent more products and services to five targeted IT-centric customers with resources who have been cross-pollinated within two years
Track sales call data in real time	Decrease the number of people required to answer RFPs from five to two within two years

Figure 5.1. Common Tactical Needs Identified Across Marketing and Sales. (*Continued*)

The numbers indicate common threads and needs across tactics in at least three places in these two OGTMs alone. The BIOs ought to be closely involved in the creation of these plans, and the similarities ought to be topics of conversation and collaboration for the BIOs associated with each. Let's explore what the substance of the conversation might be by highlighting similarities across these plans and what they might mean.

Aligning on Data-Gathering Tools

In Figure 5.1, the two tactics that are annotated with the number "(1)" both involve customer data analysis. Look first at "Develop a better means of collecting and sorting customer data," which Marketing came up with. Marketing to both existing and potential customers can be improved by first understanding what appeals to current customers, who the best customers are on the basis of metrics such as revenue and profitability per customer, and which products and services are best suited to which customers. With better sources of customer data, Marketing campaigns can be tailored. Likewise, when a potential customer is actually in conversation with the company about purchasing products or services, it is essential for the company to know what comparable customers have purchased, at what price point, and what the customers' levels of satisfaction are with the purchase. This then allows the Sales team to enter into these conversations with greater confidence that what they are selling and how they are selling it are likely to yield not only a sale but also a positive result for the customer.

Now notice that the Figure 5.1 Sales tactic "Develop tools to track customer data" is directly connected to the Marketing tactic; so the two of them belong to the same strategic thread. This leads to a practical implication and benefit for Marketing, Sales, and IT of identifying cross-functional commonalities.

Often marketing departments and sales departments, by following their strategic intentions, invest in their own solutions to aggregate the relevant data, or they use the same solution in differing ways that diminish the opportunity to identify and share insights from across the data set that have an impact on both departments. IT, as a functional area in which technology-related strategic intentions and potential solutions come together, should help reconcile this by having a series of conversations with different business stakeholders in similar capabilities to understand who would be using the tools. They should also evaluate the process to enter data into the tools and the process to analyze the data for insights once the data has been entered. This reconciliation will address the risk of redundancy (pursuing independent, although closely related technology solutions) and maximize the value that could potentially be created from leveraging tools across functions, often beyond the two functions in which commonalities and differences were noticed in the first place. In our hypothetical case, for example, the operations function might also leverage both the tool and the data generated by the tool to optimize its processes and partner or customer engagement across different parts of the value chain.

Only after cross-functional themes are identified and broader applications of a new tool are considered should IT (or anyone else) contemplate specific solutions. BIOs and the enterprise architect function (to be described in Chapter Six) each have a role to play here. Identifying these synergies early and as part of the strategic planning process increases the likelihood of avoiding redundancies, leveraging reuse potential, and realizing economies of scale before significant investments are made, and that project-based execution of the strategic opportunities will not need to be delayed. With these things in mind, it is essential to develop early the right data taxonomy before investing. Many companies do the reverse, and many wind up investing in redundant solutions. That need not be, when IT is the advisor and the shepherd in this process.

Let's look now at the next set of tactics highlighted in Figure 5.1 between Marketing and Sales, which deals in part with bundling. These are related to the set we just discussed, in that it is better data that will allow the organization to determine which products or services can provide more value to clients and more revenue to the company when they are bundled together. Bundled offerings are often creative ways to garner higher revenues from existing customers, and can lead to deeper and therefore "stickier" relationships with customers, as customers come to rely on and, it is hoped, appreciate the company and its offering more. Again, IT sees these tactics in two different plans, and understands them strategically as another opportunity to collaborate, investing once when in the past these might have been two redundant investments.

Sharing Human Resources

The third set of tactics highlighted across functions in Figure 5.1 is internally rather than externally focused—potentially yielding benefits within the company primarily rather than providing benefits to the customer. With so much value to be derived at the intersection between IT and a variety of disciplines, a wonderful development has been that some companies have begun to share human resources staff across traditional functional areas. Marketing and Sales are two departments in which these "year abroad" programs (as one of my CIO clients refers to his cross-pollination efforts) have worked regarding IT matters, since each is being transformed through the better use of information, and each is becoming much more tech savvy. The two divisions exchange team members for limited periods of time.

Also, IT should jump at the opportunity to send business-savvy technologists into business functions such as Marketing and Sales, and it should welcome technology-savvy marketers or sales representatives to spend time in IT to help develop the business perspective among the IT team members. As with any new person, the kinds of insights people participating in this cross-functional exchange will generate are more likely to be unique, as their ideas will be colored with different recent experiences. Be sure to leverage these people for insights early in their tenures before they get woven too firmly into the fabric of the division.

By the way, cross-pollination opportunities are great ways to reward deserving people who have no higher promotional path within IT. The best IT departments constantly contemplate succession planning, determining who could succeed the CIO and who could succeed each of the direct reports of the CIO from among those who report to each of them. When no one is currently a possible successor, efforts are made to train the best of the current candidates. In this way IT is never caught off guard if someone leaves the company or is promoted. Each leader should have an apprentice of sorts who can take on certain responsibilities from the more senior person when the latter is on vacation or otherwise occupied. Still, high-potential individuals may find their own advancement blocked by a successful person ahead of them who is not ready to be promoted. In that scenario, rather than lose the high-potential individual to another company, IT should instead opt to send them to a different division of the company where new experiences can be garnered, and their value to the company can be enhanced. A positive quality of high-potential individuals is their typically ambitious desire to accrue new experiences. Later, if the original position above them in IT opens up, they will have much broader experiences to bring to bear in the new role. If it does not open up, then the "year abroad" may turn into a permanent move, which will likely also be good for the company.

From Divisional OGTM Tactics to IT OGTMs

As I've already said, in many companies, strategic frameworks like the charts in Figure 5.1 would be developed by each division in isolation. Marketing would develop its plans, and Sales would develop its plans, independently, as would Finance, Operations, Human Resources, and Product and Services divisions. Often in these scenarios, the opportunity to collaborate or the opportunity to eliminate redundant investments is lost. IT has the opportunity to facilitate the necessary collaboration to ensure that a single solution is chosen to address the needs of multiple parts of the organization. In fact, a single project that addresses multiple needs across the company ought to be a higher priority by virtue of the breadth of value that can be attributed to it.

The redundancy in investment I have observed in solutions chosen by different departments in many organizations across industries is exacerbated by the ease with which some of these technology solutions can be procured. With cloud-based, software-as-a-service offerings, they appear relatively simple, straightforward, and cost effective. As a result, and often supported through technology vendors' sales pitches, the business departments may be lured into the false conclusion that IT need not be involved. As I have also noted before, it speaks volumes of the perception of IT if executives attempt to work around the department more than they work with it.

Ideally, the company will have a well-developed mission and vision statement as well as a corporate or enterprise strategy that should be the starting point for the strategic planning for all departments, including the business and IT functions. After the plans of the other parts of the organization have been developed and IT has woven itself into those plans, then IT should develop its own strategy. The IT strategy should reflect whatever is revealed in the plans of other parts of the organization. In Figure 5.1, for example, clearly there is a customer relationship management theme, a data analytics theme, and an HR theme; each is a likely starting point for an IT strategic objective or tactic.

At this stage, IT leaders should ask themselves questions such as these:

Which of the tactics developed by the business areas, such as Sales and Marketing, can be brought to life with technology?

Do the tactics articulated in the divisional strategies suggest the need for process changes? Even if divisional-level process change is not in the purview of IT, it is essential that IT understand the process changes before identifying technology to automate process. Too many IT organizations do not adequately contemplate the former, and find that they have invested in irrelevant solutions. In some cases the impact or even disruption caused by a process change may offset the potential benefits of a technology solution.

Do our existing technologies (hardware and software) allow us to achieve what is insinuated in these strategic plans? Even if the organization decides not to upgrade current technologies, the evolution and maintenance of current technologies will require some IT and business effort. Answering this and other questions as well as decision making more broadly should be about business capabilities and use cases rather than technology features.

Insofar as new technology will be needed, will it replace or even render some existing solutions obsolete? Sunsetting of these redundant systems should be planned for from the outset.

Do these needs imply skills and knowledge that we have in short supply today? Are they appropriate to grow (through training and hiring), or would it be better to engage vendor partners to acquire the skills more quickly? Would a hybrid approach be better—vendor partner supplementation in the short term with homegrown talent in the medium and long terms?

What happens to skills and knowledge that may eventually be replaced? What are the consequences for the staff associated with these—often critical—legacy skills and knowledge?

How IT Strategy Addresses Both Business and Technology

Let's take the example of mobile strategy. Mobility is a strategic area with company and customer implications whose details vary by industry. As a company's workforce increasingly operates away from a traditional office setting—working on the road, working from home, and the like—the company wants mobile solutions that will ensure that workers—wherever they may be—are as productive as they would be in the office. Likewise, customers of many industries are becoming used to making transactions or using services no matter where they are and on any device they happen to have with them. The mobile opportunity that arises with this increasing mobility will often be defined in the plans of numerous divisions, including product and service divisions, Marketing, Sales, Human Resources, Corporate Communications, and Legal.

As the transcending function that will be responsible for bringing different aspects of these mobile plans to life, IT must push for a higher degree of collaboration among the division leaders. Conversations need to take place in which each division presents to the others the opportunity it sees, so that each division will be better informed of the company-wide opportunity. With this perspective, each division will likely be more cognizant that its individual need should fit into an overall strategy, and this will ensure that a single solution or a limited number of solutions can be chosen to meet the needs of the broadest set of constituents among employees, customers, or both. In this way, IT can truly be a strategic enabler across individual divisions, pushing each division to sharpen plans related to the single mobility strategy while also fostering a greater and cross-functional understanding across the organization.

At the conclusion of these cross-divisional conversations, IT should develop its own plan related to mobility, the overarching strategic issue in this case. An IT strategy for mobile should take into account the needs articulated by each of the relevant divisions, as well as address the technological aspects that are under the purview of IT. In short, IT strategy should ideally be able to address the business and technology aspects.

For example, consider the BIO who has been assigned to Sales. Figure 5.2 shows an example of an OGTM for a single Sales objective, which the BIO has assisted in creating. That BIO should

Sales Objective	Goals (Objective KPIs)
Upgrade productivity technology for the company's salesforce	Ensure that all sales tools have mobile capabilities by year end
	Ensure that 90 percent of the salesforce leverages mobile tools on sales calls by the end of the second quarter of next year
Tactics	**Measures (Tactic KPIs)**
Invest in hardware and online tools to increase the mobile sales-force's conversion	Increase mobile-based salesforce conversion by X percent by year end
Improve sales talent	Increase revenue per sales staff by 25 percent by the end of next year
Streamline sales processes	Decrease the sales cycle time from four days to two days by year end
Provide better training for sales staff	Improve salesforce training sat-isfaction scores from 60 percent satisfied to 90 percent satisfied (as determined by the participant sur-vey) by the end of next year

Figure 5.2. One Sales OGTM.

know this OGTM and all others for Sales quite well, such that when he or she gathers with the other BIOs, the group can begin to speak cogently about the themes that are common across plans. For example, Figure 5.3 shows some objectives and tactics from various divisions, all having a mobile component. (I have simpli-fied here, omitting the goals and measures that would normally be included.) Take a moment with the tactics column, thinking about what a solid basis it begins to lay for creating powerful IT strategy.

I focus your attention on the various divisional tactics because this is the level that will become the corresponding IT objectives

Division	Objective	Tactic
Product	Develop products that reflect our customers' changing needs	Develop mobile products to reflect customers' desire to access our products or services on the go
Marketing	Develop a digital marketing campaign	Develop a mobile-enabled marketing campaign for mobile audiences
Sales	Upgrade technology for the salesforce	Develop mobile versions of the five most-used sales tools
Human Resources	Increase employee satisfaction	Provide the mobile workforce with mobile tools to make their jobs easier
Corporate Communications	Develop electronic platforms for communicating internally and externally	Develop mobile communications formats that work on any device
Legal	Reduce legal risk for the company	Develop a legal risk mitigation plan for mobile

Figure 5.3. Comparing Thematically Related Objectives and Tactics Across Divisions.

at the subordinate strategic level. (Revisit Figure 2.7 to refresh your memory about the cascade.)

Still Improving Divisional Planning for an Optimal IT Strategy Too

As you see, demand for mobile, and thus the strategic need to address it, emerges from a diverse array of constituents. Since mobile technology is the common component, this is a prime example of when IT needs to bring the leaders of the divisions together to have them fully articulate the opportunity for use of mobile that their respective tactics embody. Not so surprisingly, some of the opportunities are external (for the Product division and for the Marketing division), one is internal (HR), and three are both (Sales, Corporate Communications, and Legal). Quite likely and to some degree understandably, the difference may indicate how well each cluster (external versus internal) has considered the implications of mobile outside its main concern. For example, HR may be less concerned about the customer than the employee, but the IT leader is dealing with other constituents besides HR.

In so doing, IT leaders should develop their own comfort level with topics and ideas relevant to each division, but the BIO should be the in-depth expert of the division. As a result, BIOs should be given in-depth training in the area of expertise of the division to which they are aligned. This means having the Marketing BIO be trained in marketing disciplines, for example. It may also mean drawing IT-savvy employees from those divisions to be BIOs, as mentioned earlier, and in the process more tightly tying IT with those divisions because of the sharing of resources. In that case, it may be necessary to provide IT skills to the new BIO formerly from Marketing. In either case, promoting cross-functional expertise is likely to be incredibly valuable, leading to richer insights and faster paths from opportunity identification to solution creation.

Together with his or her BIOs and more clearly articulated plans, the CIO should understand as well or better than the division heads how the opportunities articulated in the collection of Business objectives and Business tactics (the precursor to the IT strategy) relate to existing processes and technologies, and where they suggest new processes and technologies. This is important for two reasons: first, it will likely have implications for the IT strategy, as I said earlier; but second and arguably more important, the CIO, at the business level, should help articulate what might be done commonly versus that which probably warrants a unique response. Most people think their needs are unique, and it takes a judicious arbiter to help evaluate when that is, or is not, the case.

The CIO should facilitate the conversation, pushing each of the gathered business executives to better articulate his or her needs; the nature of the opportunity; the risk of doing nothing; the people, process, and technology changes that are likely needed; and so on. The CIO and the BIOs should also have done some research and development to understand what innovative solutions exist and how other companies have leveraged them to their advantage. If off-the-shelf solutions are not available, they will also be in a position to provide guidance on the efforts and costs required to build them internally. They should also understand the pitfalls of using certain vendors or solutions, and offer that counsel, at least from a technology perspective, even if vendor management resides in Procurement or another functional area.

After this session or series of sessions concludes, everyone involved should feel they have a better understanding of the mobile opportunity as it pertains to their area of responsibility as well as for the company as a whole. The CIO and his or her leadership team should also have a clearer idea of IT's role in providing solutions that will benefit the company and its customers alike.

Example: Translating Divisional Tactics into an IT Objective

In the case of mobile, divisional tactics might translate into an IT objective as shown in Figure 5.4.

The "Sales Tactic" in Figure 5.4 corresponds with the first tactic in Figure 5.2. This is one of several tactics related to the Sales objective "Upgrade technology for the salesforce." That objective would also be one of five to seven objectives that the Sales team developed. (Generally, fewer objectives are better as long as they provide sufficient guidance.)

The IT objective, "Create a market-leading mobile platform flexible enough for company and customer use," derives from the

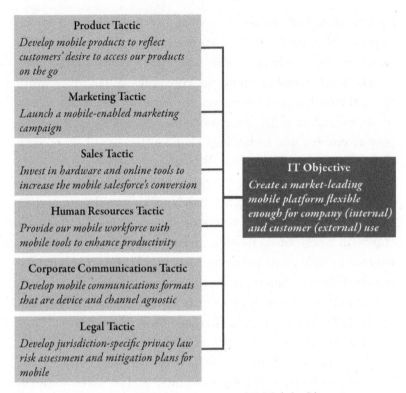

Figure 5.4. From Divisional Tactics to an IT Mobile Objective.

Business tactics developed within the various divisions. It clearly notes IT's domain, which is to develop (or purchase) the platform and to provide the technology capabilities to maintain it. Many IT departments have a bias toward purchasing off-the-shelf products whenever possible rather than designing them anew. The IT objective also pledges that IT will take into consideration the needs of the company and the needs of customers in identifying and implementing the platform. It also suggests IT's desire to limit the number of solutions that the company must design or purchase and maintain. This is also a responsibility of IT, as the divisions, if left to their own devices, are increasingly likely to purchase solutions that suit their needs alone, leaving IT to maintain several potentially redundant solutions, often increasing the cost to run IT in the process.

Please note that the strategic frameworks highlighted so far do not mention projects. It is critically important that the strategic frameworks be developed without specific projects in mind; this avoids creating strategy *around* projects or solutions. Strategy should be developed on the basis of the strategic drivers of the internal and external environment and not upon solutions that may or may not relate to these drivers. Many companies make the mistake of doing this in reverse.

Don't Let Projects Run the Show

This may appear simple, but do not take it for granted that your company currently gets this right. Working in reverse (project precedes strategy) not only constitutes a self-fulfilling prophecy but rids the strategic planning process of some of its main purposes, such as identifying opportunities and allowing for course corrections, if needed. When a strategy is created or retrofitted to justify a dreamed-up project idea that a division or the IT department wishes to pursue, the strategic planning process is shortchanged. That process ought to be about identifying broad strategic opportunities as well as filtering what *not* to pursue, not about retroactively sanctioning projects.

Focusing first on objectives and then cascading through to tactics brings a better chance that the strategic plans at the corporate, divisional, and IT levels will be aligned or integrated as well as more focused. Plans that intend to retrofit projects already approved are likely to point in many directions at once. In that case, chances worsen for mobilizing employees to push in the same direction. In addition, using a strategic framework to encourage and identify ideas will be more difficult, if not impossible. The extent to which new ideas might be solicited for tactics, for instance, is also limited because people will realize that the already-approved project idea must come first. With an OGTM like that in Figure 5.4, it is much clearer where the focus is, and in which directions new ideas for tactics might be offered.

Broad Finalization, Then Project Planning

Only after related and aligned strategic plans across business divisions and IT are finalized is anyone ready to add projects to the plans of their own division. Figure 5.5 shows IT projects aligned to one Sales division OGTM. They are the ones in italics.

The italicized projects in the figure are the ones with major IT implications. The second, third, and fourth tactics are less IT-centric, though given the process excellence that IT departments often have, it is possible that IT would be involved in implementing the projects aligned with the tactic "Streamline sales processes."

Sales Objective	Goals (Objective KPIs)
Upgrade productivity technology for the company salesforce	• Ensure that all sales tools have mobile capabilities by year end • Ensure that 90 percent of the salesforce leverages mobile tools on sales calls by the end of the second quarter of next year

Tactics	Measures (Tactic KPIs)	Current Year Projects/Features	Future Projects/ Features Backlog
Invest in hardware and online tools to increase the mobile salesforce's conversion	Increase mobile-based salesforce conversion by X percent by year end	• *Replace current sales platform with a mobile platform* • *Pilot tablets with a subset of our salesforce*	*Roll out tablets to entire salesforce*

Figure 5.5. IT-Related Projects (Italics) in Service of One Sales Objective.

Tactics	Measures (Tactic KPIs)	Current Year Projects/Features	Future Projects/ Features Backlog
Improve sales talent	Increase revenue per sales staff by 25 percent by the end of next year	• Evaluate sales talent • Work with executive recruiters to devise training programs and retire less talented sales staff	
Streamline sales processes	Decrease the sales cycle time from four days to two days by year end	• Assess existing sales processes • Develop a "to be" picture of the core sales processes • Develop a process-improvement program	
Provide better training for sales staff	Improve sales-force training satisfaction scores from 60 percent satisfied to 90 percent satisfied (as determined by the participant survey) by the end of next year	• Revise training sessions • Develop survey questions in order to determine sales-force satisfaction and competence • Benchmark satisfaction rates relative to our competitors	

Figure 5.5. IT-Related Projects (Italics) in Service of One Sales Objective. (*Continued*)

Clearly, mobile is a cross-divisional effort. It is appropriate to align projects with multiple strategic plans. At a minimum, this conveys the full importance of the project. Moreover, as has been mentioned multiple times, IT's perch in the corporate structure means that it should identify projects that have an impact on multiple parts of the organization, so IT leaders should strive to define such projects.

When an IT BIO has been assigned to a business division or function, those units will be integrally involved in the development of the IT aspects of the plan and should push their business team to develop IT-centric tactics where the BIO has identified opportunities; conversely, the BIO will also push IT to develop technology solutions with an eye toward business value-add. As the BIOs get together to discuss the plans of the divisions with which they interface, an opportunity arises to cross-pollinate new ideas and to ensure that the organization is leveraging existing infrastructure and reusing existing processes and technologies to avoid new, redundant spending wherever possible.

At Last, an IT OGTM

Figure 5.6 shows the IT mobile OGTM with projects aligned to it.

Whereas the projects that were italicized in Figure 5.5 were IT projects directed at Sales, the projects in Figure 5.6 are projects that support the organization more broadly. It is up to IT to invest in a common mobile platform for the company, limiting and focusing the necessary investment to implement it and maintain it, but it is also up to IT to ensure that the solution chosen will meet the needs of all relevant constituents.

Other topics that typically require IT-specific strategies include those for which IT is likely to hold primary responsibility:

- Security
- Risk management

IT Objective	Goals (Objective KPIs)
Create a market-leading mobile platform flexible enough for company (internal) and customer (external) use	• Limit the number of mobile platforms to one by year end • Receive at least 90 percent satisfaction by the end of next year from colleagues on ease of use of mobile solutions

Tactics	Measures (Tactic KPIs)	Current Year Projects/ Features	Future Projects/Features Backlog
Identify the best-fit platform for our company and our customers	• Receive 80 percent high satisfaction for mobile capabilities by the end of next year among colleagues and customers	• Conduct competitive mobile platform landscape analysis • Develop mobile platform RFP • Contract with a vendor • Set up a service-level agreement with chosen vendor	
Develop an integration plan for the single-target platform	• Achieve full integration by the end of this July • Attain 100 percent seamless integration with other solutions offered by our company	• Set up an integration team • Engage consulting help on the integration efforts	

Figure 5.6. IT's OGTM for Company Mobile, Including Projects.

Tactics	Measures (Tactic KPIs)	Current Year Projects/ Features	Future Projects/Features Backlog
Develop and execute a security policy on mobile solutions	• Reduce the number of attempted mobile solution security breaches by 50 percent of current baseline through the end of next year	• *None* identified due to lack of appropriate expertise	
Retire all legacy systems that will be replaced for mobile	• Ensure that no redundant mobile systems are necessary to execute core sales capabilities by the end of next year	• Develop a mobile asset management program • Execute a mobile legacy program phase-out and transition plan	• Develop a lifecycle management plan for the new tool, including regular version upgrades to avoid accumulation of technical debt

Figure 5.6. IT's OGTM for Company Mobile, Including Projects. (Continued)

- Technology maintenance and refreshment
- Service or help desk
- Business continuity and disaster recovery
- Enterprise architecture

This list is not exhaustive, and it will vary from company to company. In these cases, IT must use its strategic framework to help articulate plans as to how these topics will be managed, how they will evolve, and how they will continue to improve.

Still more strategy-worthy topics will emerge as you explore opportunities across the divisions, like the mobile example. Recent themes I've seen include ones akin to those mentioned in Chapter Two:

- Data analytics and other big data opportunities
- Social media
- Content management
- Cloud computing

Each of these has profound business implications that will be obvious to many business leaders. If those leaders do not get creative ideas from IT, they will pursue them on their own. IT needs to be so close with the divisions of the company that it can identify these needs as they emerge. Great IT teams will have already started to think about the implications of these trends before they hear from the business, having read or otherwise learned about how other companies have begun to leverage them to their own advantage. The best IT departments will develop the business case for these ideas even before the divisions of the company (or the competition, for that matter) have articulated these topics and others as opportunities. These forward-looking and innovative IT departments can make a real difference—for their business partners and for their organizations as a whole. This is the way the best IT departments become indispensable advisors to the rest of the organization.

Owning a Tactic

In Chapter Two, where I described the success metrics of strategic planning (the goals and measures of OGTM), I called them critical because what gets measured gets done. Nothing gets done, however, unless there are people responsible and held accountable for the measurable improvement. This is another area in which strategic plans sometimes fail. OGTMs or their equivalent are created, and the executive committee or the board agrees that the plan is the right one for the foreseeable future. Who is accountable or responsible for ensuring that the plan is enacted? The easy answer is that the IT strategy is the responsibility of the CIO. This is absolutely true, but the CIO cannot do it alone. He or she must work with the business leaders, as I outlined before, but also engage other leaders in IT, to ensure that the strategy is enacted. The IT objectives as the highest-level part of the strategic framework are the primary responsibility of the CIO, and the tactics are the primary responsibility of members of the IT leadership team and, in certain select cases, the rest of the company. Figure 5.7 continues Figure 5.6 by adding a column for tactic owners.

It is important to note that the people assigned in the last column are not necessarily responsible for the projects that may be needed to execute the tactic to which their name is attached. That responsibility would likely fall to project managers, there often being several projects associated with a given tactic; the people named in Figure 5.7 are responsible for their tactic, which is still part of the strategy, as a whole. Whether or not they are responsible for some or all of the constituent projects is a different consideration. Other divisions of the company should be encouraged to assign people to be responsible for tactics. Unless there is a person responsible for each tactic, they may not be accomplished in due time, and the objective will suffer in the process. The tactic owner may also be responsible for updating or otherwise maintaining the tactic. While the tactic owner usually is not—and should not be—the person responsible for strategic reviews, he or she may trigger a strategic review if circumstances dictate revising the approach.

It should be clear to tactic owners that they are also responsible for "turning the dial" in the fashion suggested by the measure. Therefore, Jack Johnson is responsible for the tactic that reads "Identify the best-fit platform for our company and our customers."

IT Objective	Goals (Objective KPIs)
Create a market-leading mobile platform flexible enough for company (internal) and customer (external) use	• Limit the number of mobile platforms to one by year end • Receive at least 90 percent satisfaction by the end of next year from colleagues on ease of use of mobile solutions

Tactics	Measures (Tactic KPIs)	Current Year Projects/Features	Future Projects/Features Backlog	Tactic Owner
Identify the best-fit platform for our company and our customers	• Receive 80 percent high satisfaction for mobile capabilities by the end of next year among colleagues and customers	• Conduct competitive mobile platform landscape analysis • Develop mobile platform RFP • Contract with a vendor • Set up a service-level agreement with chosen vendor		Jack Johnson
Develop an integration plan for the single-target platform	• Achieve full integration by the end of this July • Attain 100 percent seamless integration with other solutions offered by our company	• Set up an integration team • Engage consulting help on the integration efforts		Jill Thomas

Figure 5.7. IT's Mobile OGTM, Including Ownerships.

Tactics	Measures (Tactic KPIs)	Current Year Projects/Features	Future Projects/ Features Backlog	Tactic Owner
Develop and execute a security policy on mobile solutions	• Reduce the number of attempted mobile solution security breaches by 50 percent of current baseline through the end of next year	• *None* identified due to lack of appropriate expertise		David Adams
Retire all legacy systems that will be replaced for mobile	• Ensure that no redundant mobile systems are necessary to execute core sales capabilities by the end of next year	• Develop a mobile asset management program • Execute a mobile legacy program phaseout and transition plan	• Develop a lifecycle management plan for the new tool, including regular version upgrades to avoid accumulation of technical debt	Susan Matthews

Figure 5.7. IT's Mobile OGTM, Including Ownerships. (*Continued*)

He is also responsible for the measure that reads "Receive 80 percent high satisfaction for mobile capabilities by the end of next year among colleagues and customers." The tactic owner may determine that the existing projects aligned with the tactics do not sufficiently accomplish the measure. Not all projects move the needle on a given tactic in the same direction. He or she should solicit submissions for additional project ideas to accomplish each tactic. Of course, he or she should work with the CIO and the rest of the leadership team, as well as with the BIOs, to identify these ideas. Jack would not necessarily be responsible for each of the projects. There would be project managers for those, but he would have oversight of the tactics to ensure that they are on track. For smaller companies, it is possible that the tactic owner would also manage projects, but for larger companies, those roles are likely to be separated.

Staffing a Tactic

Next, it is important to think about how to staff each tactic. This is different from the specifics of project staffing, but at a minimum, it is important to understand whether the new capabilities that will be developed as a result of what is suggested by the tactic can be developed with internal capabilities or not. Figure 5.8 illustrates how staffing resources can be added to the planning, in this case distinguishing between internal and external sources.

In the figure you will note some tactics that can be accomplished with existing staff and others that cannot. This will especially be the case for IT departments (and companies in general) that focus on new, innovative ideas. Departments often lack the staff to carry out new ideas. In this situation it is important to contemplate whether the skills required are ones that the company wishes to grow internally or to engage from outside—the buy-versus-build decision. Of course, this may not be a black and white decision. In the gray zone in which a combination of internal and external resources are likely to be needed, that should be noted as well. Developing or growing internal skills can be costly, and it

IT Objective

Create a market-leading mobile platform flexible enough for company (internal) and customer (external) use

Goals (Objective KPIs)

- Limit the number of mobile platforms to one by year end
- Receive at least 90 percent satisfaction by the end of next year from colleagues on ease of use of mobile solutions

Tactics	Measures (Tactic KPIs)	Current Year Projects/ Features	Future Projects/ Feature Backlog	Tactic Owner	Internal Resources	External Resources
Identify the best-fit platform for our company and customers	• Receive 80 percent high satisfaction for mobile capabilities by the end of next year among colleagues and customers	• Conduct competitive mobile platform landscape analysis • Develop mobile platform RFP • Contract with a vendor • Set up a service-level agreement with chosen vendor		Jack Johnson	• No internal resources are available to lead this currently • Given its importance, need to combine training of some existing staff with recruiting new staff to fill this gap	• The solution will be delivered by an external vendor • Leverage that vendor for support for the near and medium terms while we grow • Ensure that training of our staff is included in the contract
Develop an integration plan for the single-target platform	• Achieve full integration by the end of this July • Attain 100 percent seamless integration with other solutions offered by our company	• Set up an integration team • Engage consulting help on the integration efforts		Jill Thomas	• IT integration team will lead all initiatives related to this	

Tactics	Measures (Tactic KPIs)	Current Year Projects/ Features	Future Projects/ Feature Backlog	Tactic Owner	Internal Resources	External Resources
Develop and execute a security policy on mobile solutions	• Reduce the number of attempted mobile solution security breaches by 50 percent of current baseline through the end of next year	• *None identified due to lack of appropriate expertise*		David Adams	• Our security team has no mobile capabilities currently • Hire a new director of mobile security	• Hire a vendor partner to help lead this tactic until internal capabilities have matured appropriately
Retire all legacy systems that will be replaced for mobile	• Ensure that no redundant mobile systems are necessary to execute core sales capabilities by the end of next year	• Develop a mobile asset management program • Execute a mobile legacy program phase-out and transition plan	• Develop a lifecycle management plan for the new tool, including regular version upgrades to avoid accumulation of technical debt	Susan Matthews	• Those managers who are responsible for each system to be retired should lead their retirement	

Figure 5.8. The IT Mobile OGTM, with Staffing.

may mean adding head count. If the tactic suggests a potential source of competitive advantage, or if it will simply be more efficient to have the core resources be employees, then it is best to plan this way from the outset. Still, some skills are best provided and managed by vendors for the foreseeable future, for example, when it is unclear how long they will be needed and whether the opportunity they support will be long term or not.

Tactics Currently Lacking Projects

You may have noticed in Figure 5.8 that no project is attached to the tactic "Develop and execute a security policy on mobile solutions." Actually, it is generally a good sign when there are tactics with as-yet-undetermined projects; it means that some creative new thinking has been going on. This, by the way, is another reason to develop the strategic framework prior to and independent of the projects: to identify white space opportunity. If there are projects supporting every tactic, one wonders whether the truly creative new ideas have been identified among the tactics.

Note that the gap for the security policy tactic is annotated "*None* identified due to lack of appropriate expertise." This suggests the need to leverage outside experts to help identify project ideas. Depending on how your organization defines what constitutes a "project," there may be other reasons why a tactic may not show a project. There are certain things that may be strategically valuable but that can be achieved outside of a project. For example, ongoing collaboration or communication that reach a significance beyond day-to-day interactions may rise to the level of strategic significance, in effect implementing a tactic.

Constituents outside the company must be engaged as a key source of innovative ideas. Not enough CIOs have adequate access to the company's customers. CIOs ought to engage customers to help devise new ideas because customers know the company's products and services best, and presumably are prepared to purchase the products and services that will emerge through innovation.

Regarding IT's external partners, too many CIOs view them as ful-
fillers of work exclusively rather than tapping them for their broad
sets of experience to develop new, innovative ideas on the company's behalf. The best external partners (true partners as opposed
to simply vendors, mind you) may know your business best from
partnering with you over the years. They may understand your
strengths and weaknesses nearly as well as the CIO does, and they
likely have a wide array of experiences in your industry and in
related industries. Tap them effectively for insights, and you will
be ahead of most other CIOs the world over.

By laying out your strategic plans as clearly as you see in Figure 5.8,
you place the onus on good external partners to deliver new project
ideas and possibly even additional tactic ideas that align with your
specific OGTMs. External partners who do not have access to these
plans either because they do not exist or because the plans are kept
too close to the vest are forced to propose new ideas that are to some
degree guesswork. As a result, the external partner may be accused
of proposing what is best for the external partner rather than for
the company or the IT department. Granted, some strategies, such
as the desire to acquire another organization or to expand business
areas, may need to be kept confidential, but many aspects of strategic
plans become more powerful when shared with partners that can
help execute them. By sharing this level of detail with them, when
appropriate, you remove misunderstanding and make clear to external partners that whenever they propose new ideas, they need to be
crystal clear about how those ideas will help advance some aspect of
the strategic plan. This helps eliminate wasted time and effort, and
it engages a much broader community of strategic contributors in
pushing ideas forward.

Other Strategic Frameworks

While my firm and I use the OGTM as a strategic framework,
the general method of strategic planning can align with another

strategic framework you or your company might favor. Here are two examples of how other frameworks can serve much the same ends for IT in its own and broader strategy work. The first is from Procter & Gamble and looks immediately very much like OGTM. The second is from Ecolab, where the framework looks different on the outside but fundamentally parallels OGTM in the essentials.

Procter & Gamble and OGSM

Functionally and geographically, Filippo Passerini took a circuitous route to the CIO role at Procter & Gamble. Beginning in his native Italy, he rose through the ranks from junior positions to senior-most ones at P&G's world headquarters in Cincinnati, Ohio. He started in IT, but also spent time in marketing and operations roles before becoming CIO.

Hoping that IT will run as a typical business function, P&G has a history of hiring CIOs who have traditional business experience. Passerini continued this tradition, and in 2005, as CIO, he led the integration of Gillette. In 2008, Passerini was also named the president of Global Business Services, and in 2011 he was named group president of Global Business Services. Given the breadth of experiences Passerini has had across a variety of businesses, functions, and geographies, he never thought of IT as anything less than a strategic part of the business. In fact, he argued, "All leaders need to think of their areas as strategic and value enhancing to the business, or else they will be underperforming by definition."[2]

One way in which IT and Global Business Services have creatively harnessed the power of IT has been by creating digital "war rooms" across the globe, assembling an assortment of leading-edge analytics capabilities to enable the $84 billion colossus to make better decisions through insights drawn from across geographies, product segments, business functions, and the like. Therefore, his organization has managed the "big data" conundrum as well as any organization in the world. What sort of strategic planning process uncovered this war-room idea as an area of opportunity?

Figure 5.9. OGSM Compared with OGTM.

P&G employs a model called OGSM, an acronym strikingly similar to OGTM (see Figure 5.9). Both derive O, G, and M from objective, goals, and measures, and use those terms in about the same way. Rather than tactics, the "S" stands for "strategies." The similarity is reinforced also in the fact that in OGSM, as Passerini likes to simplify things, "the 'O' and the 'S' are words, and the 'G' and 'M' are numbers."

Passerini made the point that objectives at the highest level are not necessarily surprising. At that corporate level, they center on things such as revenue growth, cost efficiencies, and geographic expansion. P&G's objectives are likely to be broad enough that they will not change for a few years. Likewise, the goals and measures are somewhat straightforward because they offer feedback on how far to go and how fast, so to speak. The goals are "just a number," he said, helping to articulate how far and how fast the company should push to accomplish the objective. Of course, he hastened to say, "choosing the right number is essential."

The strategies, he said, are the more complicated part because, "Strategic planning is about making choices. A world of opportunity is before us, but we need to decide where to focus our attention. Once our choices are made, we know where to focus the attention of our 129,000 people." In addition, the strategies should change more often, in some cases annually, though some may be relevant for several years.

Where and How to Win

The methods that P&G uses to create its strategies are covered well in the book *Playing to Win: How Strategy Really Works*, coauthored by P&G CEO A. G. Lafley. It describes the need to decipher "where to play" and "how to win." Passerini says the "where to play" question should be answered by the objectives, and "how to win" should be answered by the strategies (the tactics of OGTM). The book holds several key insights, such as

- Strategy is about making specific choices to win in the marketplace.
- Optimization is not strategy.
- Winning should be at the heart of any strategy.
- There is no perfect strategy.
- Make the consumer the boss.
- Measure everything.[3]

The focus on "winning" rather than simply optimizing what the company already has is key to how Lafley and his colleagues operate. It may not be so surprising to note that P&G's CEO thinks in this way, but it speaks volumes that Passerini and his team do, too. Historically among IT leaders, optimization has been their area of greater strength, and Passerini and his team certainly do much to optimize processes, and to automate what has traditionally been handled manually. But to a much greater extent, he and his team think about the *new value* they can create in order to help the company achieve its broader objectives to win in the marketplace.

The book's discussion of its key insights raises many other interesting points, but I'd like to skip now to the last. As I said earlier, "that which gets measured gets done," but too often plans are put in place without a reliable definition of what the *destination* is. In those cases, it is much more difficult to determine whether the team has been successful or not. In P&G's methodology, as in the one

I've used in this book, the goals and measures are key to ensuring that there *is* a well-defined destination and that the percentage of achieving it (incomplete or complete) can be determined.

Playing to Win: How Strategy Really Works also goes on to note that, in developing strategic plans, executives must be able to answer the following questions:

- What is your winning aspiration?
- Where will you play?
- How will you win?
- What capabilities must be in place?
- What management systems are required?[4]

In Strategy Planning, Is Size a Disadvantage?

Some people think of size as a hindrance to making better decisions. Large companies are often thought of as being bureaucratic, slow, and conservative. Certainly, there are many companies that fuel this stereotype. P&G is not one of them. Passerini has thought about the advantage of size. From the vast number of products P&G has flowing through most countries on earth and all the different consumers in those various places, P&G collects a tremendous amount of information on its products and its customers. This can be harnessed to get a better picture of who, right now, is buying what and why, but it can also help in making better decisions about consumers' future buying patterns. This has an impact on marketing plans, sales plans, and product launches, among other areas. Passerini understood that this is the advantage of being large and broad, and he has determined how his part of the company, fueled by IT, can help P&G "win."

Ecolab and VSEM

Ecolab is a St. Paul, Minnesota–based $13 billion revenue developer and marketer of solutions and on-site service for the food, health care, energy, hospitality, and industrial markets in more than 170 countries around the world. The company provides cleaning and sanitizing, food safety, infection prevention, pest elimination, water management, and energy conservation products and programs, as well as equipment maintenance and repair services, to commercial customers. The company has been a tremendous success story in the past decade, growing substantially both organically and through acquisition.

In mid-2011, Ecolab announced that it would acquire Nalco, a company that specialized in chemistries and solutions for industrial water and air applications, for $5.38 billion.[5] When the deal was official in December of 2011, Stewart McCutcheon was promoted from Nalco's chief information and productivity officer to Ecolab's executive vice president and CIO.

In taking over IT for the larger company, seeing cultures, methods, and technologies that needed to be harmonized, McCutcheon realized he needed a better way to plan. He utilized a process called VSEM that, like OGSM, is also similar to OGTM. The acronym captures its four facets: vision, strategy, execution, and metrics. Like the OGTM, there is a cascading logic to the framework. Two essential patterns are to move from high-level principles to granular tactics and to attach measurement that ensures things stay on track. Figure 5.10 provides the definitions of the facets of VSEM.

The framework is equal parts a time-oriented map, as it were, that plots a course today through to the foreseeable future, and a communications framework for making clear to colleagues across the company where IT will contribute value to the corporation. McCutcheon said, "It is essential that we have a common vocabulary and process for setting and measuring goals and objectives throughout the organization. The clearer our plans, the more we can mobilize all of IT to accomplish our goals."[6]

This is an essential point. The less clear plans are, the more people will push in different directions. When employees do not work toward a common goal, at best they waste time and money.

Vision	Long-term look at future aspirations (3+ years)
Strategy	How to make progress toward vision (2 to 3 years)
Execution	Goals to support strategies (12 months)
Metrics	Measure results to provide team and personal accountability

Figure 5.10. VSEM.

Source: Stewart McCutcheon and Ecolab.

At worst, through lack of focus they fritter away opportunities and are beaten by competitors with greater strategic clarity. The better that employees understand what the next twelve months through three years and beyond is supposed to entail, the more solid ideas they can develop to help drive the plans forward, and the more satisfied they will be, understanding the connection between their day-to-day tasks and the greater vision of the organization.

To further clarify the intent of each leg of the VSEM framework, I've filled in Figure 5.11 with some of the actual information from one of McCutcheon's recent plans.

The VSEM term *vision* is equivalent to an OGTM *objective*. The vision captured in the figure is one of a set of four that work together. The other three visions refer to growth, productivity, and customer and associate engagement. The one shown here is certainly grandiose. It declares that the organization is shooting to be the best, not just in the industry, but beyond, and that its performance should be felt by a diverse array of constituents, from customers to colleagues within the company.

A VSEM *strategy* begins the qualifying process. Equivalent to an OGTM *tactic*, it clarifies by stating that some of the IT team's focus needs to be to "deploy valuable business solutions." This suggests a filter through which to run any contemplated new solution. Planners are pushed to ask, "Does this proposed solution represent

Common vocabulary and process for setting and measuring goals and objectives throughout the organization	
Vision	We aspire to be the best IT team in the world, providing superior value to every Customer, Business, Region, and Function
Strategy	Deploy valuable business solutions
Execution	Increase the use of standard business solutions globally
Metrics	Equip sales-and-service employees with next-generation mobile solutions improving productivity

Figure 5.11. One Recent VSEM.

Source: Stewart McCutcheon and Ecolab.

a valuable solution for our business?" That question points to the need for IT to understand the rest of the organization sufficiently in order to give an accurate answer.

If projects were aligned with this strategy directly, leaders might infer that it would be appropriate to invest in technologies that are expensive, and to err on the side of purchasing or creating solutions that perfectly meet the needs of the constituents, since one can certainly argue that that would be of great potential value. Therefore, VSEM's *execution* statement (in some ways like a more granular *tactic* in an OGTM) qualifies the strategy further by pointing out a need to "increase the use of standard business solutions globally." This articulates a bias toward minimizing the solutions portfolio wherever possible. One good reason for this is that IT bears the brunt of the heavy lifting when solutions are tailored to specific needs.

In addition to the statement pictured, there are two other execution statements:

- Focus on growth, profitability, engagement
- Accelerate solution deployment using Scrum, Cloud, and Virtualization

Since that which gets measured gets done, *execution* statements must be coupled with appropriate *metrics*. With these fully articulated, only then are project ideas formulated and documented. There are three that connect to the execution statement and metric noted:

- Enable integrated supply chain planning and execution
- Expand and accelerate the enterprise resource planning footprint
- Scale standard field and commercial solutions

Linking IT Strategy with the Strategies of the Rest of the Organization

I hope that it is clearer now how IT strategy and the strategy of the rest of the divisions and the companies all fit together. I also hope that it is clear that the CIO is well situated to lead the company in this way. Achieving strategic alignment across the company is a noble goal, and one that the CIO is in a good position to undertake. In so doing, the CIO will also glean insights that will help ensure that the right projects are chosen to achieve the highest value across the company.

A better-engaged IT department is likely to have a clearer understanding of how IT projects align across the plans. Each completed project adds to the portfolio of technologies that IT must manage. This is yet another black box that IT must emerge from. Enterprise architecture, the topic of the next chapter, is an ideal way to better understand how each new project fits or does not, and how the architecture that IT manages needs to evolve in order to support the plans of the company. This is another key element to the strategic planning process that IT manages and must communicate with colleagues across the company.

IT Strategy Take-Aways

1. As CIO, start by listening.

2. Use a broadly shared strategy framework to map, align, and document strategic planning. (Here, we've used the terminology and format of OGTM.)

3. Dedicate IT business information officers (BIOs) to continually collaborate with individual divisions.

   • Their eyes and ears should focus on adding business value.

   • Convene your BIOs to share, cross-pollinate, and spot redundancies.

4. Send IT leaders to other divisions on internal "years abroad," and offer the same to other functions.

5. From the tactical needs of other divisions, explore cross-functional IT business and technology possibilities, including common threads that can align the company on things such as data-gathering tools and shared people resources.

6. Assist other divisions in creating their OGTMs (see also Chapter Four). Urge them to postpone defining projects until corporate and other parts of the company have also reached that stage.

7. Devise IT's OGTMs as cascades from corporate and divisional tactics.

   • Take corporate and divisional tactics and measures as starting points for creating IT objectives.

   • Answer the questions: Where can technology work best? Are changes needed in process or in your current hardware and software?

8. Continue helping divisions improve and coordinate the business value of their OGTMs.

9. Bring divisional leaders together to articulate and compare shared themes, opportunities, and tactics.

   • Be a facilitator, pushing everyone to better articulate needs; the nature of the opportunity, the risk of doing nothing; the people, process, and technology changes that are likely needed; and so on.

   • Help them understand each other's perspective.

10. Understand more fully how the opportunities articulated in the business objectives and business tactics outside IT relate to existing and potential processes and technologies.

11. Develop IT OGTMs for divisions (and their shared interests) and for supporting the organization more broadly.

    • Invest in common platforms. Limit and focus investment needed to implement and maintain them.

    • Ensure that solutions meet the needs of all relevant constituents.

    • Among your OGTMs, also address areas for which the IT department is primarily responsible.

12. Assign an IT owner to every IT tactic.

    • Distinguish that role from that of a project manager.

    • Weigh advantages of developing the capabilities to achieve each tactic with existing or new internal or external human resources.

13. Engage partners outside the company as sources of new ideas.

6

Enterprise Architecture

Chapter Four described how IT can help itself by helping the company and its divisions generate their strategies in a way that enables IT to create a strategy of its own that prioritizes and supports the divisions' various objectives in a coordinated and efficient way. Chapter Five highlighted the method of using those inputs to formulate IT's own strategic plan. Both of those steps may still leave unclear how strategy at all levels connects with the material resources that IT manages in terms of hardware, software, and applications. To bridge that gap, this chapter describes a concept called "enterprise architecture" (EA) that helps to ensure a tight tie between strategies and IT tools and solutions.

Generally speaking, a company's IT enterprise architecture is its configuration of IT material resources in service of the interests of business strategy. It forms a blueprint, noting what technology the company currently has and guiding how future technology investments will fit into or change what currently exists.

A company's IT enterprise architecture is a holistic design for an organization, aligning the current-state IT capabilities, processes, and resources to enable business strategy; it provides a foundation to guide the ecosystem's future-state evolution to continually adapt to and operationalize the business strategy.

It is important to note that EA can refer to a function and a series of outputs, but is also the name of the team that heads the function, which can cause some confusion. The Chief Information Officer (CIO) Council is the principal U.S. government interagency forum for improving practices in the design, modernization, use, sharing, and performance of federal information resources. The CIO Council defines EA as the function that should translate an enterprise's business vision of the "future state" into effective enterprise change. The Council refers to the EA as the "glue" that ties business and IT strategy together and that allows them to drive each other.[1] A clearly articulated EA is an essential part of any IT strategic plan.

The IT department must think about how each of the requests from the corporation, from the divisions, and that IT itself suggests through its own plans fit with what is already in existence. As a process, enterprise architecture involves clarifying whatever configurations of IT hardware, software, data, and applications already exist and maintaining an overview and rationale of that configuration in order to control its change. Starting from a *baseline architecture* of what currently exists, the EA process works out a *sequencing plan* that will lead to a new, *target architecture* in line with future strategies and mission.

Your EA knowledge base should document the present state of your technology and the planned future state, and it should be structured well enough to provide the head of EA and the CIO the ability to counsel those inside and outside of IT on what is feasible and what changes are necessary in order to achieve feasibility.

By documenting and managing its EA, an IT department can ensure that systems, applications, and data seamlessly fit and work together in a way that is scalable and flexible. After all, unless a company is a true startup, each new tactic or project suggested in the strategic plan means that some of the systems, hardware, processes, and even people may change.

I'll continue here with an overview of the EA process and the people involved, using the company Red Hat as an example. After that I'll provide examples of how two other companies created and maintain their enterprise architectures. EA information complements the information in the divisional and IT strategies.

There are different ways in which EA can be captured or integrated into the IT strategic framework, as I will explain later. There are already terrific resources about EA and its tie to strategy, perhaps the best among them being *Enterprise Architecture as Strategy* by Jeanne Ross, Peter Weill, and David Robinson.[2] My brief description in this chapter follows on great work such as theirs.

On average, IT departments tend to be better when it comes to developing new capabilities; they tend to be worse when it comes to shutting down old applications, software, and hardware. EA provides the framework through which better governance of all that IT managers do can be sorted out, and it helps ensure that as new capabilities are brought to bear, the ones that they are supposed to replace do not remain as costly and unnecessary redundancies. Just as with the broader and higher-level strategies, EA is not static and evolves as strategic drivers and needs change.

Four Facets of Enterprise Architecture

The best way for IT departments to conceive and manage their enterprise architecture function is by dividing it into four facets or domains:

> *Business architecture.* The business architecture reflects the strategic plans at the enterprise (in other words, company-wide) and the divisional levels. The OGTM is the connection point function: clarify, elaborate, and illuminate the business model to define opportunities, and provide a foundation for creating a cohesive business operating model.
>
> *Information architecture.* The data architecture defines data relationships and the appropriate data sets themselves that the company employs to feed business strategy and optimization decisions. Data architecture is the basis of application design and delivery.

Application architecture. The application architecture encompasses the range of applications that the company buys or builds and integrates.

Infrastructure architecture. The infrastructure architecture encompasses all the IT elements that the organization leverages to operate day in and day out. It also takes into consideration the tools and processes to monitor and manage these IT elements.

Together, these four facets help ensure the short- and long-term effectiveness of delivering business technology solutions that enable efficient, effective, responsive, and agile business operations.

The relationship between enterprise-wide strategy, the four facets of EA, and the business and technology solutions architecture is shown in Figure 6.1.

Too often, these architectural elements are created without a framework or a broader vision in mind. For example, many hotels are operated by franchisees. Although many of the major players

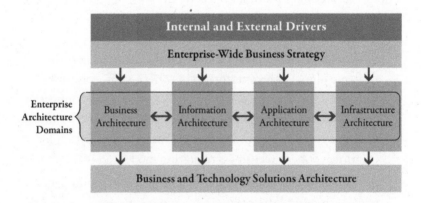

Figure 6.1. How the Four Facets of EA Relate to Enterprise-Wide Strategy and Drive the Creation of New Solutions.

Source: The four EA domains in the graphic are taken from Randy Heffner, "Updated 2010: The Pillars of Enterprise Architecture Terminology," *Report for Enterprise Architecture Professionals* (Cambridge, MA: Forrester Research, 2010).

have developed a common database providing a single view of the customer, there are still a number of companies that have not tied this together. A common business architecture would provide a single branding synergy. A common data architecture would provide a greater ability to cross-sell to customers on the basis of enhanced knowledge of what pleases them. Without such, insufficient thought is put into why the architectural elements have developed and how to optimize them. The cascading logic from strategy to the technology that the company will invest in should be defined. Figure 6.2 shows the cascade, depicting the logical connection point between business strategy and EA.

Leadership is needed to look after a company's EA—either an individual or a team of "architects"—usually called the "enterprise architect." Enterprise architects sit at the intersection of

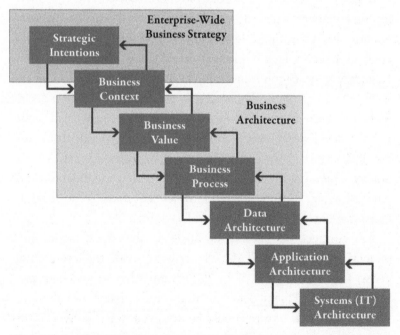

Figure 6.2. The Cascading Connection Between Business Strategy and Enterprise Architecture.

strategy and technology, and they should be considered equal parts business strategists and technologists. This is one of the few non-C-level positions that should have a holistic view of the company, translating plans to processes, information, and information technology assets.

Creating an Enterprise Architecture Function

The reasons to develop an EA function are many. Various massive, multibusiness unit companies have done so in order to set better standards and to govern more from a central authority. Others recognize that the ever-hastening pace of change in technology requires an ability to understand rapidly how each change will affect existing architecture. Many companies seek each of these advantages and others. Some have created an EA function in hopes of rendering IT's operation more transparent, thus facilitating collaboration across the enterprise. Still others want a systematic way to evaluate how technology is evolving so that the company's technology is relatively fresh. Others, still, hope to leverage EA in order to ensure that the technologies they adopt are flexible and reuseable. The process of establishing EA often begins with the creation of a cross-divisional committee that will facilitate the development of a roadmap tied to strategy and, ultimately, the decisions that need to be made to update the company's technology. This cross-divisional collaboration is a wonderful benefit of establishing an EA function, and this level of transparency leads to more shared accounting for what IT is doing.

EA connections need to be made to objectives, tactics, and projects within the OGTMs. Objectives provide the overarching vision for the company or IT department that should help provide structure to make decisions that have impacts over the long term. Also, the EA team should be involved in the conversations that generate tactics and projects, so it can share its perspective on what is currently in existence that can be used to fill a need articulated by a tactic. Also, this team should advise the rest of IT leadership and the leadership beyond IT about those aspects of the strategy that will not be realistic with the current technology. This may not mean that a path can't be taken, but it may mean that the path will be much longer than anticipated. The EA team should note where needs are emerging in multiple plans, thus identifying opportunities to make single investments that will have an impact on the broadest part of the organization.

At its most fundamental, the process to establish an EA roadmap requires several steps. The first is getting a comprehensive snapshot of the current state of technology. What hardware, software, applications, and data does IT have under its control today? Knowing that current state is essential to understand what is possible. The IT strategy may be unrealistic if it is not cognizant of the current state of IT.

Next, it is important to determine what the various strategies at the corporate level, at the divisional level, and within IT dictate in terms of change to the current state.

Then the gap between the current and future states must be filled. It is up to the EA team to come up with the options in both design and sequencing, and to ensure that the company is pursuing the right opportunities.

The EA Team

Different companies refer to the roles within IT slightly differently. Red Hat is a $1.5 billion company offering open source software solutions, using a community-powered approach to develop and offer operating system, middleware, virtualization, storage, and cloud technologies. EA is especially important in a company that has products which are technology-based and that draws upon a wide array of partners inside and outside of the company to develop those products. EA is a way in which the IT department can sort through what may seem like a chaotic web of plans. Lee Congdon is Red Hat's CIO, and has been very active in refining the IT department's EA capabilities.

Red Hat has an enterprise architecture role and three additional roles that interact with the enterprise architects:

- The *enterprise architect* has the responsibility for architectural design and documentation at a landscape and technical reference model level. The enterprise architect often leads a group of the segment architects, the solution architects, or both, related to a given program. The focus of the enterprise architect is on functions required by enterprise-level business.[3]

- The *segment architect* has the responsibility for architectural design and documentation of specific business problems or organizations. A segment architect reuses the output from all other architects, joining detailed technical solutions to the overall architectural landscape. The focus of the segment architect is on enterprise-level business solutions in a given domain, such as finance, human resources, sales, and so on.[4]

- The *solution architect* has the responsibility for architectural design and documentation at a system or subsystem level, such as management or security. A solution architect may shield the enterprise or segment architect from the unnecessary details of the systems, products, or technologies. The focus of the solution architect is on system technology solutions; for example, a component of a solution such as enterprise data warehousing.[5]

- *Domain architects* focus on a specific domain and have deep expertise in that area. Typically, these architects only focus on specific areas. Examples of these include business architect, security architect, information architect, infrastructure architect, communications architect, and so on.[6]

To describe the differences between these roles, Congdon offered the chart captured as Figure 6.3, which differentiates each role on the basis of product, function, and service or interaction.

The architecture review board mentioned in the figure is a governing body for EA involving the head of EA and his or her team, and often the CIO; its meetings may be attended by a variety of people outside of IT when appropriate and relevant. It is this body that is ultimately responsible for creating the EA plan, typically, and for enforcing compliance with the EA strategy whenever new project proposals are made. They may grant exceptions, but it is up to the person or members of a division requesting an exception to justify noncompliance, as opposed to the EA justifying why the division leaders must adhere to the standards set in the EA plan. Architecture review boards occasionally have the reputation of being bureaucratic, and therefore it is important to be clear on the important objectives of this body at the outset of its creation so that its value is not in question and people do not make their best efforts to circumvent it.

To better explain the ways in which these roles fit together and within the corporate structure, Congdon offered the content captured in Figure 6.4.

This provides an appropriate context for the roles. Enterprise architects encompass roles that align to the facets mentioned earlier with some nuances based on Red Hat's unique needs. They are

- Business architect
- Data architect
- Security architect
- Applications architect
- Technology architect

As mentioned earlier, this group has the broadest purview, as the "enterprise" title would suggest. They work directly with

	Enterprise Architect			Segment Architect	
Function	**Service or Interaction**	**Product**	**Function**	**Service or Interaction**
• Architecture review board member	• Consulting to domain, segment, and solution architects. • Architecture approval • Architecture governance • Standards setting • Consult with domain architects	• Segment roadmaps	• Architecture review board member	• Consulting to solution architects • Segment governance • Consult with domain and enterprise architects

	Solution Architect			Domain Architect	
Function	**Service or Interaction**	**Product**	**Function**	**Service or Interaction**
• Project team member	• Project architecture and design • Consult with domain architect • Accountable to segment architect • Liaise with architect governance	• Architecture pattern • Technology evaluations • Technology roadmap • Reference architecture	• Architecture review board reviewer	• Consulting to solution, segment, and enterprise architects • Consult with enterprise architects

Figure 6.3. EA Roles.

Source: Lee Congdon and Red Hat.

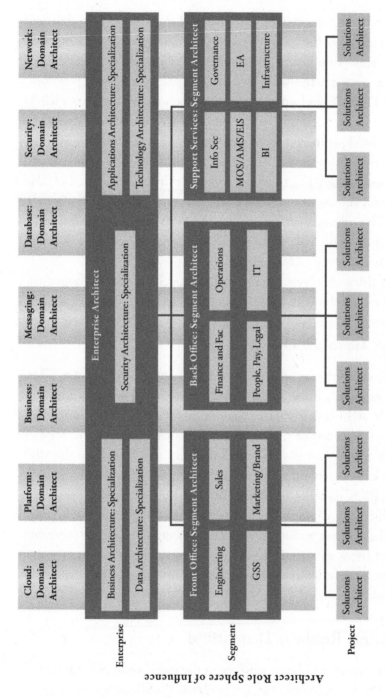

Figure 6.4. The Relationship of EA Roles with Other Relevant Architecture Roles.

Source: Lee Congdon and Red Hat.

segment architects, who are divided into areas of expertise and alignment on the basis of front-office functions or segments such as Engineering, Sales, and Marketing or Brand; back-office functions or segments such as Finance and Facilities, Operations, and IT itself; and support services functions or segments such as Information Security, business intelligence, and infrastructure.

The domain architects own topics such as cloud, messaging, security, and network. They are deep in these topics, and remain abreast of the needs of the company in these areas, but also remain abreast of the latest trends in these areas.

The solutions architects draw upon the inputs from the other functions, and work to develop the appropriate solutions, leveraging the existing architecture wherever possible.

I think this breakdown translates nicely into most companies, and is a solid way to think about divisions of labor and expertise.

The Tie to the OGTMs

The enterprise architects should be familiar with all OGTMs, but especially those at the corporate or enterprise level. The segment architects should be familiar with the OGTMs of the different divisions of the companies. In other parts of the book, I refer to the business information officer (BIO). Where the BIO role exists, segment architects will likely work hand-in-hand with the BIOs in order to ensure that nothing is missed. Enterprise architects and segment architects should seek out the counsel of the domain architects when an objective, tactic, or emerging need aligns with their respective domains. Finally, solution architects are most likely to ensure that the projects that support tactics are aligned with the overall EA.

The EA Roadmap Demystified

For many of my clients who are in the early stages of contemplating the development of an EA roadmap, the challenge can be quite intimidating. As you will see in an example later in this chapter, EA documents can be quite visually complex, and even more complex to gather together. Under the leadership of CIO Lee Congdon and EA manager Eric Brown, members of the Red Hat EA team put together a presentation (leveraging sources as diverse as the U.S. government's "Federal EA Consolidated Reference Model Document" to a site that provides input on running half marathons) to "demystify" the creation of EA roadmaps.

Matt Stuempfle, an enterprise architect on the Red Hat EA team, indicated that enterprise roadmaps are key to answering the following questions:[7]

- Where are we going?
- How do we get there?
- When will we get there?

He noted that it is important to be intentional, making informed decisions and knowing the consequences of those decisions. He indicated that Red Hat defines a roadmap as "a sequenced series of interrelated activities and outcomes required to achieve a defined set of related objectives designed to influence and drive the business." That is a nice definition, and describes why EA roadmaps are a key outgrowth of the strategy processes of the prior chapters. Note the emphasis on defining "objectives" and focusing on how to achieve them. I also like the focus on the sequence, which reminds us that a worthy objective will take several steps to achieve and also that it is important that these steps be interrelated so that none of them takes the team off course and steals precious time.

Stuempfle went on to define three key words and illustrate them with easily understood examples:

Objective. A high-level statement that articulates what we want to accomplish. ("I want to be physically fit before going to the beach.")

Outcome. A measurable value delivered and associated with an objective. ("Lose fifteen pounds by the end of April.")

Activity. The actions or work that we take to achieve an outcome. This is the "how" we get there. ("Create an exercise plan." "Exercise sixty minutes today.")

Continuing with the same example, Stuempfle said that "one must begin with an objective." He defined this in a comparable fashion to how we have defined objectives as part of the OGTM throughout this book. In this case, he provided the example of "'I want to be physically fit.' Therefore, the roadmap is the complete physical improvement plan—from meals to exercise to mental well-being—properly balanced and sequenced to achieve my goal and sustainability."

Figure 6.5 provides an overview of objectives, descriptions of those objectives, and milestone outcomes. As you read through this, I hope you'll see linkages to the objectives and goals of the OGTMs.

To commence the development of the roadmaps, Red Hat's EA leadership team recommends mapping activities to activities first, activities to outcomes second, and outcomes to outcomes next. Figure 6.6 offers an example of this using the same physical fitness example.

It is important to plot as many steps in the map as possible. Focus mostly on the interdependencies between inputs and outputs. As you do so, you will naturally uncover necessary changes in sequencing.

Note that projects are simply plotted on this graph without a real thought as to how far to the left or right projects ought to be. Stuempfle pointed out that this could lead to a bias of one item or another on the basis of its relative isolation on the chart making it easier to read. He suggested using automation to take out this potential "bias," thus equalizing where different items are plotted across the roadmap. To equalize the chart according to projects

Objective	Description	Milestone Outcomes
Exercise	Incorporate exercise in my daily routine to drive overall well-being	**Phase 1.0** Complete a half marathon in under 2.5 hours as a concrete demonstration of physical stamina, resilience, and physical and mental well-being **Phase 1.0** Reduce my resting heart rate to 60 bpm when averaged at random intervals over a four-day period
Weight	Reduce my weight to within healthy standards	**Phase 1.0** Lose 10 pounds by August 1 **Phase 1.0** Lose 20 pounds by September 1 **Phase 1.0** Lose 25 pounds by November 1
Diet	Eat better	**Phase 1.0** Increase the variety of foods in my regular diet by 25 percent **Phase 1.0** Reduce the average cost of work lunches by 20 percent

Figure 6.5. Objectives and Outcomes.

Source: Matt Stuempfle and Red Hat.

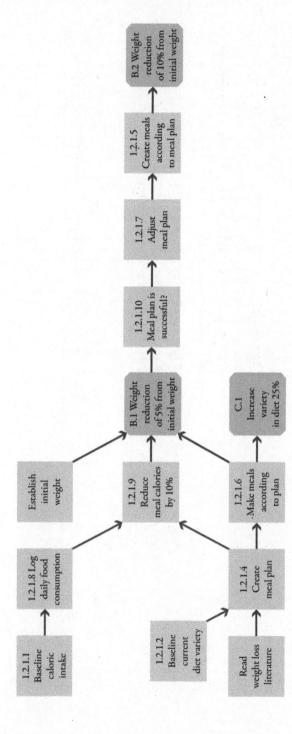

Figure 6.6. The Initial Map.

Source: Matt Stuempfle and Red Hat.

that have more or fewer dependencies, Stuempfle suggested nar-
rowing the chart, and changing its representation a bit, as shown
in Figure 6.7.

Figure 6.7 offers a comprehensive view evening out the spac-
ing between items on the roadmap. The plotting is solely based
on dependencies, and does not have the potential disadvantages
of manual plotting shown in Figure 6.6. Red Hat EA leadership
emphasizes that an assumption for the next phase of the chart
is that the team should only do work that provides measurable
value within a given time period. This is provocative in many
IT departments, where value is not adequately evaluated on a consistent basis, but this becomes a great forcing function to ensure
that discipline is in place. To do this, Stuempfle groups phases
by their *outcomes*, as shown in Figure 6.8. Through this harmoniz-
ing process, true priorities and a logical sequence emerge.

Now we can see more distinct time windows, prioritization of
outcomes, and the impact of that prioritization. This real-world
example illustrates the basic building blocks for putting together
a roadmap.

Let's turn now to two more extended examples of IT departments that have adopted an EA approach.

EA at Cardinal Health

Cardinal Health is a $100 billion health care services company
providing pharmaceutical and medical products and services that
help pharmacies, hospitals, ambulatory surgery centers, clini-
cal laboratories, physician offices, and other health care provid-
ers. Prior to 2004, the company did not have a company-wide
IT department. Rather, the divisions (several of which were the
size of *Fortune* 500 companies) had their own IT departments and
their own CIOs. Those CIOs operated autonomously with little
influence across divisions, and there were no company-wide IT
standards to adhere to.

The early 2000s was a period when the concept of service-oriented architecture emerged as a best practice, as leading IT leaders began to think more about how to leverage technology more broadly and manage IT to be more efficient. Cardinal Health was part of the zeitgeist during this period. In 2003, the largest of Cardinal Health's divisions—Pharmaceuticals—elected to create an applications architecture team. The team was instructed to set applications standards, the goal being to reduce costs and garner efficiencies within the Pharmaceuticals team, a division of the company in which standards had not been the focus. In 2004, once the Pharmaceuticals segment team showed progress in this effort, Cardinal Health created a company-wide IT department. One driving consideration was the company's tremendous collective buying power, which it no longer wanted to squander by inefficient practices. At the time, myriad vendors were doing the same things across multiple divisions of the company. About 70 percent of the collective budget of IT was being spent on what might be termed "keeping the lights on." In other words, the vast part of IT budgets wasn't serving innovation. One of the tasks of the nascent company-wide IT division was to be more forward looking, and that meant increasing the percentage of the budget dedicated to innovative activities.

Steps at Cardinal Health

One of the early steps on this journey was to define Cardinal's enterprise architecture. It began with the development of an architecture review board (ARB), under the leadership of Brent Stutz, the company's first director of applications architecture with a newly formed EA team. (Later a vice president as well, Stutz would lead the function until June of 2013, when he became senior vice president of commercial technologies, chief technology officer of Cardinal Health.) The ARB led to greater engagement of business unit IT leaders across the company than was previously possible,

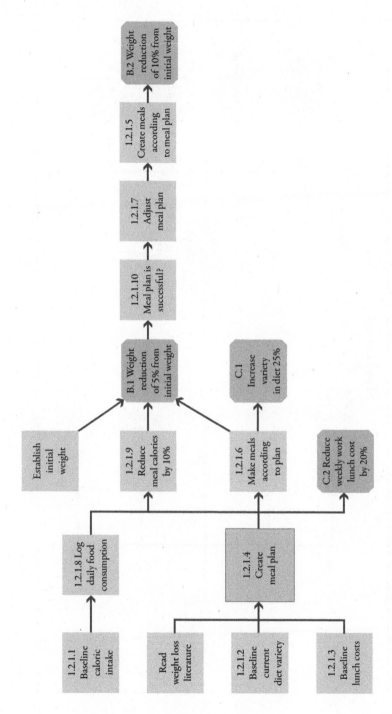

Figure 6.7. The Directed Graph.

Source: Matt Stuempfle and Red Hat.

Shape Legend

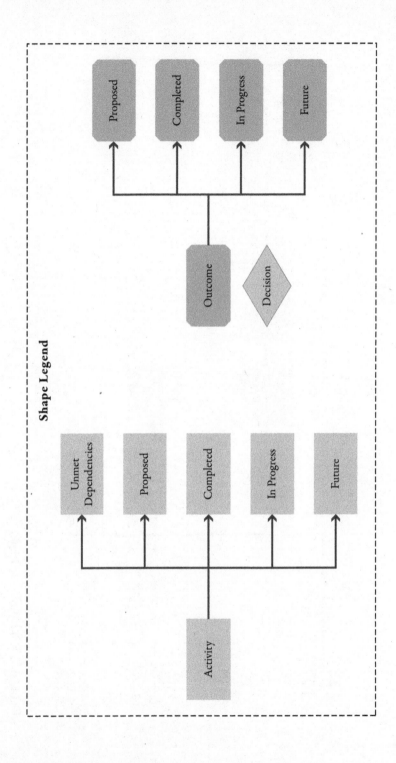

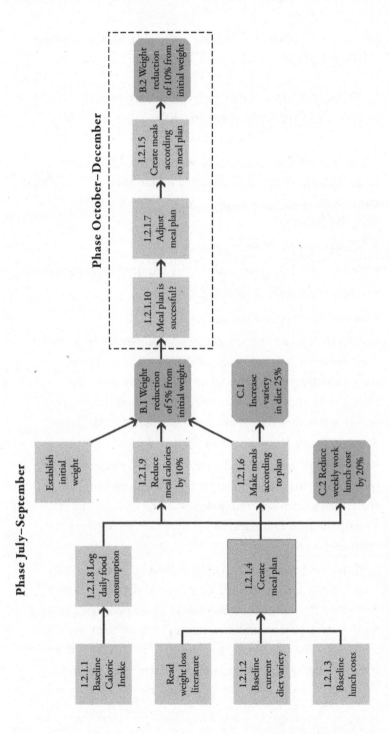

Figure 6.8. Phase-Grouped Map.
Source: Matt Stuempfle and Red Hat.

bringing them together with a regular cadence for the first time. The ARB undertook several steps:

1. It tabulated all the systems and technologies that the company had currently. Next, the ARB developed a list of costs relative to each, where applicable.

2. It sent out what was referred to as a "service class question-naire" to inquire about the relative importance of the different systems under IT's control. Among the details requested were the following:
    -   Which systems were revenue generating
    -   What availability was realistically required for each system
    -   Disaster recovery protocols for systems
    -   Fault tolerances for systems

    Results showed a natural tendency among divisions to rank their systems higher on some of these parameters than seemed logical, but this problem was mitigated by the board's having collected knowledge of costs: that cost data came in handy as a way to force executives to make tougher, more discriminating decisions about their rankings.

3. Service levels were defined for each system, ranging from 1 (not warranting an architecture) to 4 (possibly requiring an embedded architect). These designations enabled the ARB to estimate how many architects they needed for the EA team they were assembling.

4. Architectural roles that had been embedded in the various divisions of Cardinal Health were banded together under a clearer overall technical career track. Many people applied for these attractive jobs, and a particularly strong team was assembled. A few data architects were hired from outside of the company, but other than those people, the track was staffed almost exclusively by existing Cardinal Health IT people.

This was great because internal recruits already understood the company's IT issues and resources, and, critically, these people already had the trust of colleagues inside and outside of IT and they could immediately influence team members outside of the EA function.

5. To make up for lack of EA experience, thousands of dollars were put into a training curriculum, and everyone who was to make up the new enterprise architecture group went through it.

Organizing the EA Team

Cardinal Health decided to organize EA by disciplines similar to the four facets I outlined earlier, each having its own leader:

Business process. The business process architecture leader leads IT strategy, including mergers and acquisitions.

Applications. The applications architecture lead is responsible for maintaining the applications layer, noting changes to existing applications, additions of new ones, and when old ones should be turned off.

Data. The data architecture lead is responsible for contemplating the data needs and ramifications articulated in the plans.

Infrastructure and technology. The infrastructure and technology leader is responsible for the hardware, such as the networks and servers.

Cardinal Health would add a fifth facet, security. The five are highlighted in the content in Figure 6.9, providing both definitions and deliverables for these five facets.

Especially as a company grows, it is important to have someone individually responsible, ultimately, for each layer. Recall that corporate and divisional strategies fuel project demand. In turn, the projects entail various changes to various combinations of business

	Security	Infrastructure	Data	Applications	Business Process
Definitions	Defines the security and control requirements necessary to protect the confidentiality, integrity, availability, and accountability for each of the other layers of the enterprise architecture.	Defines infrastructure components upon which applications can be built, ported, and integrated in order to support the business processes of the enterprise.	Defines the enterprise structure and processes required to manage the data content, quality, and usage. It also provides the data structures and their relationships that describe how Information supports the business processes.	Defines the way in which applications are designed and how they interact. Applications architecture enables an enterprise to achieve a high level of systems integration, maximize the reuse of components, and enable the rapid deployment of applications in response to changing business requirements.	Defines the enterprise by documenting business functions. Business architecture exposes a true picture of what our business does. That allows IT to quickly automate these processes accurately and find synergies.
Deliverables	• Project-based logical security plans • Portfolio planning current-state assessment and future definition • Reference architectures (conceptual security designs and standards)	• Project-based logical infrastructure plans • Portfolio planning current-state assessment and future definition • Reference architectures (conceptual designs)	• Project-based logical data models • Portfolio planning current-state assessment and future definition • Reference architectures (conceptual designs) • Enterprise data model	• Project-based logical application models • Portfolio planning current-state assessment and future definition • Reference architectures (conceptual designs) • Application retirement list	• Specific BRITS deliverables • Current-state assessment and future-state business • Business capability framework • High-level process modeling

Figure 6.9. **Cardinal Health's Technology Domain Definitions and Deliverables.**
Source: Cardinal Health.

process, applications, data, and infrastructure and technology. Without close oversight of each layer, tremendous redundancy can arise in each layer as new capabilities are constantly added and as older technologies that should be rendered redundant by the new developments are not shut down.

The Value of Cardinal Health's EA

When Stutz contemplates the value that EA has brought to Cardinal Health, he sees two primary themes. The first theme is reduction in direct costs and head count. Direct costs shrink through the elimination of redundant capabilities, and the development of more technologies that can be reused. Fewer people are needed, especially in scenarios in which the EA function is a conglomeration of architects from across the divisions of a large organization; to serve the central EA function takes fewer staff than was required by scattered arrangements.

The second value theme is efficiency. Stutz said, "It is difficult to nail down the specific dollar figures we have saved using enterprise architecture, but our ability to make faster and better decisions because of the transparency that EA provides means that our IT operation is much more agile as a result."[8]

EA at NetApp

Based in Sunnyvale, California, NetApp is a *Fortune* 500 provider of storage systems and data management solutions for information technology infrastructures. In the latter half of the 2000s, NetApp IT was not operating well. Frequently, projects failed by any of the classic measures of timeliness, budget, or value. As a result, IT was losing credibility with the rest of the organization. To win back the trust of the rest of the organization, it needed to deliver what it said it would deliver, and to do that it needed to improve dramatically at gathering requirements, estimating costs and time, delivering, and showing the value of what was delivered. It also needed to communicate better at every stage of the work.

As a deeply technical company, NetApp made and continues to make great demands on its IT department. When this case study begins, around 2010, the company revenues were $4 billion and the goal was to increase that rapidly to $10 billion. Thus something more than a new "software development lifecycle" was needed in order for IT to improve and square up to its role. IT needed to raise itself to a level of sophistication that would serve it well, even when NetApp more than doubled its size. NetApp's CIO was and is Cynthia Stoddard. As she saw the challenge in retrospect, "We did not want to simply say we were going to do things; we wanted to prove to our colleagues that we could get it done."[9]

Again We Start with Listening

To tackle the problem, in 2010 Stoddard came up with a basic but effective plan. First, her team would map out the current-state architecture. It would be done piece by piece, while they remained always cognizant of the ultimate destination. Second, the future state would be plotted, with thoughts on eliminating redundancies, modernizing aspects of the architecture, and the like. Third, the gaps between the current state and the future state would be plotted, with ideas on how to bridge the gaps. Last, a full roadmap would be created. The key underpinning of all of this was strong governance practices, which I will describe in more detail.

To get a better idea of the current state, Stoddard and her IT executive team went on a listening tour, speaking with the vice presidents of Marketing, Finance, Sales, Operations, and Supply Chain, and the heads of the various business units. The tour gave them a lot of valuable, candid feedback from the rest of the organization. As others in the organization saw things, IT was fragmented. For example, IT personnel were developing some things for Finance while other IT personnel were doing other things for Marketing, and neither group knew what the other was doing. The IT team did not facilitate understanding and collaboration across the business silos as they should have been doing, nor were they apparently noticing or calling attention to opportunities to address multiple needs in unified ways. The best news was that IT was viewed as a *potential* source of better collaboration across the company, but it needed to find a way to turn potential into fact. As a result of the listening process and more work on their own, Stoddard and her colleagues reaffirmed the need for enterprise architecture.

An EA Forum

To begin to distill a basic roadmap, Stoddard convened what IT called an enterprise architecture executive council (EAEC). This was a forum for business partners and those IT team members who were aligned with each of the divisions of the company to come together to talk about demand from each silo, needs, opportunities, and issues faced. First and foremost, by fostering greater collaboration among these team members, the EAEC facilitated more understanding and collaboration across IT, and by extension, across the business as well. Stoddard noted, "This would become the new way to prioritize all of IT's activities and to make funding decisions, and it allowed us to do it in a transparent way."

The EAEC continues to this day. It is made up of the vice presidents of

- Marketing operations
- Sales operations
- Order processing and fulfillment
- Supply chain operations
- Finance operations
- Human resources operations
- Product operations
- Internal audit

It also includes Stoddard as CIO, two VPs of IT (one of whom chairs the council), and the senior directors of customer support operations and legal operations. This cross-section of the company meets monthly, but also can meet more frequently when opportunities are ripe. At times it even meets more than once a week. Overall, it is one of the best-attended meetings that IT hosts.

Documenting and Appraising the Current State

In 2012, NetApp hired Jonathan Kissane as chief strategy officer. For the corporation, Kissane developed a three-year plan. This plan has facilitated a greater degree of alignment between IT's plans and those of the entire company. Since then, on the basis of a combination of the annual and longer plans, IT has begun to maintain what is typically a twelve- to eighteen-month forward view, and this is the view that its enterprise architecture team leverages.

Stoddard and her IT team also have leveraged EA for a more comprehensive view of business processes. This was a substantial improvement over how things had been done before. In the past, IT would begin to automate a process for one part of the organization and pursue that effort to the point of having consumed a lot of time and money, only to discover at that point that various other processes (perhaps in other parts of the organization) would also be affected. This would lead to rework and additional time and money spent.

To counteract such problems and to begin to map things as they currently stood, the NetApp IT team implemented a methodology to highlight capabilities in three categories of systems with an aim to set standards to a greater extent:

- Systems of record
- Systems of innovation
- Systems of differentiation

This derives from Gartner's Pace-Layered Application Strategy framework.[10] Within each set of systems, various capabilities were then identified and tagged with the colors red, yellow, or green.

Red capabilities were those whose current inadequacies impeded the company's progress toward its $10 billion revenue goal. Yellow were capabilities whose level was not an impediment, but that were not propelling the company forward either. Capabilities tagged as green were the ones that the IT organization judged as highest value and supporting or even driving growth.

The color coding soon became a tool by which the company could more readily prioritize activities. The idea was to focus on the red-zone capabilities. In addition, NetApp leaders agreed that, whenever process changes were proposed, if the technologies and applications were listed as red, needed changes would be made to red items before any process change was started. The logic, the means of communicating and prioritizing, and the graphs (with the red, yellow, and green system) all worked toward an end of rendering IT's methods transparent.

Roadmapping a Future EA

Today as Stoddard and her team develop an enterprise roadmap, they align with Chief Strategy Officer Kissane's plans. At the same time, Stoddard is a member of the extended staff of NetApp CEO Thomas Georgens. Insights from these interactions and others help her team maintain a solid evaluation of the current state of technology compared to how it will need to evolve to meet the future state entailed by constantly evolving plans.

Out of this has come a gap analysis process that provides IT with an effective way to understand where it needs to develop new capabilities in order to propel the company forward via the strategic plans of the corporation and its divisions. The initial roadmap must be constantly updated on the basis of these changes, reflecting the plans articulated by the rest of the company, and the updating process needs to continually engage executives from across the company. Fortunately, after several turns at this sort of analysis, an IT department begins to develop a muscle memory of sorts, and learns how to address needs more quickly.

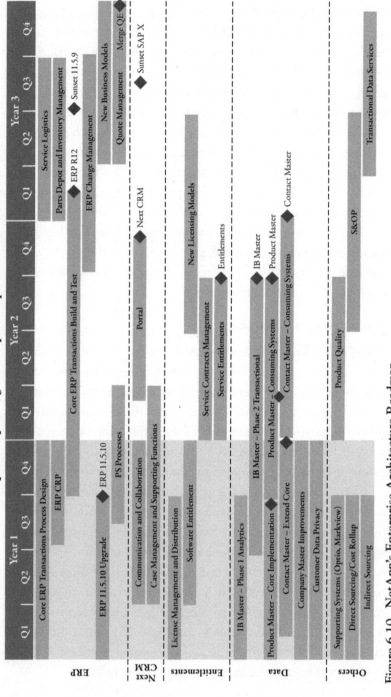

Conceptual Sequencing of Enterprise Capabilities for the Three Years

	Year 1				Year 2				Year 3			
	Q1	Q2	Q3	Q4	Q1	Q2	Q3	Q4	Q1	Q2	Q3	Q4

ERP
- Core ERP Transactions Process Design
- ERP CRP
- Core ERP Transactions Build and Test
- Service Logistics
- Parts Depot and Inventory Management
- ERP 11.5.10 Upgrade
- ERP 11.5.10
- ERP R12
- Sunset 11.5.9
- ERP Change Management
- PS Processes
- New Business Models
- Quote Management
- Merge QE

Next CRM
- Communication and Collaboration
- Case Management and Supporting Functions
- Portal
- Next CRM
- Sunset SAP X

Entitlements
- License Management and Distribution
- Software Entitlement
- Service Contracts Management
- Service Entitlements
- New Licensing Models
- Entitlements

Data
- IB Master – Phase 1 Analytics
- IB Master – Phase 2 Transactional
- IB Master
- Product Master – Core Implementation
- Product Master – Extend Core
- Product Master – Consuming Systems
- Product Master
- Contact Master – Extend Core
- Contact Master – Consuming Systems
- Contact Master
- Company Master Improvements
- Customer Data Privacy

Others
- Supporting Systems (Optio, Markview)
- Direct Sourcing/Cost Rollup
- Indirect Sourcing
- Product Quality
- S&OP
- Transactional Data Services

Figure 6.10. NetApp's Enterprise Architecture Roadmap.

Source: NetApp.

As Georgens remarked on the results of these efforts at NetApp:

> Too often CIOs have been focused on cost cutting to
> such a dramatic degree that they and their teams become
> disconnected from how the company actually creates
> value. Cynthia and her team have become embedded in
> our operation and can effectively see change through.
> Speed is the key to business success, and IT must be set
> up to deliver things at the highest speed possible.[11]

The fruit of the team's labor was the development of an actual visual roadmap. Figure 6.10 provides a recent iteration of the three-year plan.

Again, the specific items in the chart are not as important as what is plotted. There are five categories that items are mapped to: ERP, NextCRM, Entitlements, Data, and a catchall Other category. The initiatives associated with each are plotted in these categories and against time.

More Holistic IT Planning

As NetApp's enterprise architecture function has evolved, the IT organization has been able to plan more holistically according to priority, sequencing, and business value. This is done by focusing on five points:

1. *Known pain points.* To identify known pain points, Stoddard and her IT team evaluate current capability gaps through a comparison of the current state and what the strategy of the organization articulates as future company plans. IT must then determine the impact of capability pain points and manual workarounds, as well as the impact of complexity in business processes and systems.

2. *Business growth.* The IT executive team must also evaluate the pace of business growth, in order to scale IT ahead

of business growth and acquisitions. This also requires identifying breaking points and end-of-life systems.

3. *Operational inefficiencies.* By focusing on operational inefficiencies, the organization can more readily identify similar or duplicated capabilities across NetApp, and analyze corporate impact and business value.

4. *Business model changes.* Business model changes are also a reason to contemplate new activities that may require changes to the IT strategy and its related EA. Business model changes may result from an acquisition, emerging markets for the company to pursue, further globalization of the business in general, and the like.

5. *Compliance.* This is a big factor when IT contemplates how to prioritize its activities. It needs to ensure that the company is in compliance with relevant regulations and is cognizant of relevant privacy policies, and that all which it develops and maintains is secure.

The sequencing of opportunities identified among the five concerns can be determined in various ways. At NetApp, IT follows these guidelines:

- Address urgent business priorities early.
- Fix master data across the enterprise.
- Group and consolidate common capabilities: retire bolt-on systems as capabilities become available. Minimize new capabilities in systems that are candidates for retirement.
- Identify activities that can run in parallel, that give incremental business value, and that head toward end-state architecture.
- Identify activities that can simplify core upgrades (ERP, CRM).
- Consider vendor support expiration and business continuity.

EA Governance and Staffing

Key to all of this is strong governance. IT's program management office (PMO) maintains a six-quarter roadmap. By planning out eighteen months, everything from financial resources to human resources to vendor considerations can be addressed well in advance of the actual commencement of projects. Within IT, an EA review board works in concert with the PMO to help make changes quickly to the rolling eighteen-month plan as necessary.

As I noted, Stoddard is a part of the CEO staff and the EAEC, along with other functional councils. From those positions, she provides much of the translation between the different levels of the organization, and she can more readily translate needs into potential solutions and inform the rest of the EA team of changes that will be coming down the pipeline soon.

Stoddard has a staff of roughly fifteen IT people on the EA team—a good size that she is careful not to expand too hastily for fear that it could become bloated and slow. Generally speaking, the team members have two roles, one that is business discipline focused (for example, HR, Finance, Operations), and one that is technology focused (for example, big data, collaboration technology). They focus extensively on collaboration, keeping each other informed of needs that can be addressed collectively across the organization. The BIO plays a similar role and often works in concert with members of the EA team.

The Enterprise Architecture Payoff

The benefits of EA have been profound at Red Hat, at Cardinal Health, and at NetApp. In the latter case, the IT department that had a reputation for not delivering much on time, on budget, or on value has substantially changed that perspective. NetApp's IT has proven to be both more transparent and more accountable for all that it oversees and to the business that it is a part of. This has built substantially more trust in IT, and as a result, IT is called upon to get involved in many more strategic activities than it would have been only a few years ago. The executive leadership has a much clearer understanding of what IT does, and it has bought into the value that it has created.

Remember that the overarching benefit of creating and maintaining an enterprise architecture is that it helps IT enormously as IT creates its own strategy out of the strategic needs of corporate and company divisions.

EA Take-Aways

A company's IT enterprise architecture is a holistic design of an organization that aligns the current-state IT capabilities, processes, and resources to the enablement of business strategy, thereby providing a foundation to guide the ecosystem's future-state evolution to continually adapt to and operationalize the business strategy.

1. From the EA perspective, start by documenting a *baseline architecture* of what currently exists; from there, work out a *sequencing plan* that will lead to a new *target architecture* in line with future strategies and mission. Within IT, create an EA team of "enterprise architects."

   - Make one individual the head of EA, responsible for seeing that your enterprise architecture stays fresh and accurate in its current descriptions.
   - Estimate how many "architects" your EA team will need. Keep it small enough to move quickly.
   - Recruit internally from people who know the current state.
   - Train your enterprise architects.
   - Embed specific members of your EA team with specific divisions, and otherwise nurture communication.

- Organize your team so that members are responsible for layers or areas of expertise.

- Get EA team members collaborating, informing each other of needs of one part of the company that might be addressed by solutions already in place in another. (See Chapter Five for ideas about a "business information officer.")

- Devise career tracks related to the role of enterprise architect.

2. Structure your EA in a way that enables you and your head of EA to counsel those inside and outside IT on what initiatives are feasible and what changes each entails. Use your EA knowledge as a complement to the information in divisional and IT strategies.

3. Create a cross-divisional committee or forum to facilitate developing and updating an EA roadmap tied to strategy. Take divisional objectives and tactics and projects as starting points for new ideas about how a future EA should look.

4. Get a comprehensive snapshot of the current state of technology: IT's current hardware, software, applications, and data. Conceptualize an EA in terms of four cascading domains, from enterprise-wide business strategy to

- Business architecture (from outside IT)

- Data architecture

- Application architecture

- Technology architecture

5. With informal talks and structured questionnaires, survey the company to find out what people think of IT in general and of the relative importance of the different systems under IT's control. Here are some considerations: Which systems generate revenue? Realistically, what degree of availability does each system need? What are the disaster recovery protocols? What fault tolerance can each system endure?

6. Inform yourself on what systems and technologies are being used throughout the company as well as their related costs. (Use cost information as you steer divisional leaders toward clearer decisions about priorities). Determine what the various strategies at the corporate level, at the divisional level, and within IT dictate in terms of change to the current state.

7. Identify gaps between the current state of IT's EA and its future needed state.

   - Set criteria for priorities and levels of IT service that filling gaps requires. (Use this information in planning what resources IT needs.) Service levels can range from a low end of "not warranting an architecture" to a high end of "possibly requiring an embedded architect."

   - Consider NetApp's approach of red, yellow, and green tabs for prioritizing capabilities.

8. Explore other maxims for how the EA team will go about its work:

   - Speed of IT response matters.
   - Work from knowledge of "pain points."
   - Know where and how your company is growing so you can scale IT ahead of business growth and acquisitions. Stay abreast of pending changes to the company's business model.
   - Identify and address operational inefficiencies.
   - Fix master data across the enterprise.
   - Group and consolidate common capabilities. Identify activities that can run in parallel, that give incremental business value, and that head toward end-state architecture.
   - Identify activities that can simplify core upgrades (ERP, CRM).

- Identify breaking points and end-of-life systems. Retire bolt-on systems as capabilities become available. Minimize new capabilities in systems that are candidates for retirement. Consider vendor support expiration and business continuity.

- Stay abreast of compliance requirements.

9. Substantiate the value of your EA in terms of reductions in head count or direct costs, efficiency improvements, scalability, and business agility, among other possibilities.

7

Reviewing, Refreshing, and Communicating Strategy

I s strategy more art than science? As with innovation, many people think that strategy is largely a result of inspiration. The truth is that there is as much science to the process as there is art. It requires a disciplined process driven by time and events. From IT's perspective, strategy also requires that IT have resources in the room at the earliest points in the conversation when strategic plans are in formulation at the divisional level, since IT should have a role in shaping those plans. The substance of those plans should shape the strategy of IT. This logic extends to the corporate strategy as well, and, fortunately, an increasing number of CIOs report to CEOs.[1] Thus they are likely to be involved in the formulation of the strategic plans at the corporate level.

Once IT has a strategy, it needs review and adjustment as events unfold; it needs also to be communicated.

Reviewing and Refreshing Strategy

Both time- and event-based reviews are needed. Strategic plans begin with a certain set of assumptions about

- The company
- The economic environment
- Customers
- Employees

- The company's product and service offerings
- The product and service offerings of the competition
- The legal and regulatory environment
- Other factors

Strategic plans reflect the assumptions at a point in time. To ensure that plans remain relevant, especially for companies in which the pace of change is fast in any important respect, nimbleness in reflecting on those changes in the strategic plans is that much more imperative. For example, in the technology sector, software companies must stay constantly abreast of the competition, since a major possibility may exist that a competitor's compelling new product could lead to a switch away from their current line. In such environments, strategic reviews should happen more frequently and perhaps a bit less formally. That said, it is no less important to have a solid plan in place, and it is just as important to undertake a more exhaustive review at least once a year.

The refreshment of strategy is also more important with smaller, less mature players when the company's footprint and the stickiness of the product or service offering is not likely to be at the same level as a larger, more established player. An advantage for the smaller, more nimble players is they are likely to be able to enact changes in strategy more quickly than the bigger ones.

The hazard for larger, more established players in industries with a slower pace of change in the variables just listed is to become strategically lazy. Several years ago, I collaborated with IT and non-IT executives from a property and casualty insurance company. The company was one of the largest in the industry, and it had an impressive client base in most U.S. states. It had a sophisticated grasp on business operations and could fairly accurately predict what revenues would be for several years. When my colleagues and I worked on a strategic planning exercise with them, we discovered that aspects of the plan they currently followed were ten years old. In some sections in the plans, the language was literally irrelevant, so much so that I should say they were operating *in spite of* the plan—paying lip service to it at best. As we concluded our strategic planning exercise with the company, we emphasized the need to keep these plans fresh.

Often a reason for the laziness is that the traditional competition is largely made up of other large, mature organizations, which are also moving at a slow pace. Increasingly, everyone's competition may be made up of small, nimble players who wish to compete with only a slice of the overall portfolio of products or services. If you consider only the most obvious competition relevant, it is quite possible that you will suffer from a thousand cuts from smaller, nimbler, more innovative, and more hungry competitors. Entrepreneurs will find competing with aspects of strategically lazy companies all the more compelling.

Events That Should Trigger Review

Certain types of events are logical triggers for refreshing company and divisional strategy:

> *Mergers, acquisitions, and takeovers.* Adding a new company—its people, processes, technologies, products, and services— naturally means that the parent company is different than it was during the last strategic review, whether in small or significant ways.
>
> *Divestiture.* Divesting a division of the company or a product or service area also means that the company is different from the last review, and plans should be rethought.
>
> *Leadership changes.* These are issues of business continuity. For example, continuity may be threatened by the fact that the most recent strategy assumed a certain now-departed leader's ability to drive a change on which the strategy depended. Optimally, companies should have succession plans in place

should a key leader leave the company, so that the plans might largely remain as is. However, strategy must be reviewed with major leadership changes.

Reorganization. If divisions are combined, for example, then the divisional strategies need to be combined or at least rethought, as the sum of the parts may require a different plan. The same goes for divisions created from what once was a single division. By definition, this would mean that two divisional plans are necessary where once there was one.

Technology changes. Technology has a way of eliminating manual work, and can even lead to changes in personnel or the way in which current staff members do their jobs. New technology products also could lead to new market opportunities. In other ways as well, technological change could lead to the need to rethink strategic plans.

Economic downturn. Optimally, all companies have a worst-case scenario in place, especially if rain starts to fall on the economy. The response to the economic malaise that commenced across the world in earnest in 2008 is an example. Even at that point, a staggering number of companies and industries continued to operate as though the assumptions of prior years would continue ad infinitum. All plans should take into account the possibility that the economy might change, and the assumptions baked into strategic plans should be flexible as a result.

Legal or regulatory changes. It is increasingly important to monitor how legal or regulatory changes might affect a business. The Affordable Care Act's impact on the health care industry in the United States is a great example. Even though the changes it could enact are not settled, it is crucial that companies in and serving the health care industry have plans in place for the changes that the Act could bring about.

Natural disaster. Disaster recovery is one of the key disciplines that IT departments should own, but strategic plans for the corporation, divisions, and IT may need to change on the basis of different disaster scenarios such as hurricanes, tornadoes, fires, and the power outages brought about by these and other natural phenomena.

These may seem obvious as changes that lead to a need for change in a company's plans. Yet many executives do not take the time to review plans even when such major events occur. In such a scenario, executives either are operating *against* plans that to some extent do not reflect reality, or they are not operating against plans to any great extent at all. Either scenario is troubling.

Time-Based Triggers

In the absence of unsettling events, however, it is still important to schedule reviews of plans. Even if all of the assumptions from a prior year appear to be in place, a worthwhile simple exercise is to ask questions of a broad set of constituents:

- What are we doing well?
- Where should we improve?
- What opportunities do you foresee?
- What are the main threats we face?

Frankly, it is also important to take stock of what has been *accomplished* over the past year. These accomplishments may mean aspects of the last plan are complete, and they may also suggest new areas that need to be reflected in a new plan. All of this suggests the need to at least tweak plans on a regular basis.

Time-based reviews should be at least annual. They would logically link to the budgeting cycle, since the strategy ought to be the precursor to the development of a portfolio of potential projects that, in turn, provide a perspective on what money should be spent. Many leading companies hold them even more frequently, aligning to IT roadmapping, various management committee or IT investment council meetings, board meetings, or PMO reviews, or even triggered as part of post-project reviews.

Combining Time- and Event-Based Reviews

Event-based reviews are likely to lead to objective and tactic changes, whereas time-based reviews are more likely to lead to tactics changes alone. That said, the reverse can certainly happen. This is further reason to delve into the situation in either case to see precisely what changes are needed in a plan. Figure 7.1 gives an overall review of triggers for refreshing strategy related to various business units.

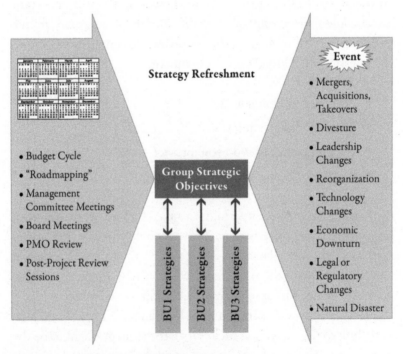

Figure 7.1. Strategy Refreshment Triggers.

The illustration does not mean, however, to suggest that strategic reviews should happen *all* the time. That would be impractical, and the return on the time spent would be marginal at best.

Communicating Strategy

Organizations often make the mistake of developing plans that are esoteric to the majority of their members. In contrast, plans need to be stated in a form that people in the specific division or another part of the company, or even those who are new to the company, would easily understand.

It is also important that there be continuity between plans. The previous section highlighted the need to update and refresh plans. As those changes are communicated, it is important to highlight what has changed from the previous iteration and why. These plans ought to be communicated with thoughts about the individual whose tactics are no longer on the map in mind. Will he or she understand why what has been focal historically no longer is? Was it because the tactic was accomplished? Was it because it was no longer relevant? If so, why? Was it because a competing tactic became of greater priority? If so, why? This highlights the need to weave themes and stories into the plan.

Create a Communications Framework Equipped for Change

Chapter Three dealt with creating a mission for IT. In Chapter Five, you read about Filippo Passerini, the group president of Global Business Services (GBS) and CIO of Procter & Gamble. Six thousand strong, GBS provides more than 170 services, including IT, finance, facilities, purchasing, and employee services as well as business building solutions for P&G's 120,000 employees in 70 countries. How does one develop a strategic plan for such a diverse organization and ensure that it translates (literally and figuratively) around the world?

It begins with a mission that is clear and concise: "To transform the way business is done." A mission of transformation points out to everyone in GBS that business as usual is not acceptable. It also implies and highlights that today's success does not guarantee tomorrow's success, and therefore new, innovative ideas must constantly be dreamed up. It establishes change as part of the mission. As Passerini said,

> Change continues to be a big part of our strategy. We need to anticipate what we believe the future will be, and seize opportunities, place some bets, and trust each other. When we began this journey, it is not something I would have anticipated unfolding so well, but it is our embrace of change that has led us to be considered perhaps the most progressive organization in the world.[2]

An Evolving Communication of Strategy

Let's follow GBS's journey from its creation in 1999. At that point, Passerini oversaw a strategy to "create shared services" to bring together separate organizations that would be more effective together than alone in delivering business services to the company. This involved

- Service consolidation
- Centralization of basic infrastructure

These were the main thrusts of the strategy through 2002.

In 2003, the organization declared a next stage of the plan to create shared services. The new objective, "Build a progressive business model," would enable GBS to focus more fully on services that provide a distinctive value and advantage to the company. This involved

- Strategic sourcing with external partners
- Running services as businesses
- Business service and IT integration

This plan was followed through 2005.

In 2006, GBS identified a need for "agility, flexibility, and change anticipation." The supporting points of this new objective were designed to increase the team's capacity, including

- Dramatic IT-driven innovation
- Ever-greater reduction in costs
- A threefold increase in organizational capacity and work throughput

In 2010, a new strategy was formulated under the banner, "GBS—Running Simpler, Flatter, Faster." The key highlights to this plan were

- Focus on key audiences: employees, functions, and business units
- More dynamic identification of priorities
- Scaled capabilities to build, operate, and deliver GBS services

Most recently, in 2013, GBS became hyperfocused on helping P&G gain a competitive advantage and win with consumers. This means working toward the company's highest business priorities. Figure 7.2 shows how Passerini and GBS depict these priorities.

These priorities demonstrate the multiple directions that Passerini and his team must contemplate. First, note the emphasis on "one [GBS]." It is important that Global Business Services operate as a single team, delivering consistent service around the globe. This consistency requires developing standard processes, standard technology, and the aforementioned ability to foster and absorb change.

Second, there is a need to foster strong business capabilities. This is particularly evident with the analytics that GBS facilitates to enable the company to make better decisions faster, irrespective of the geography that the company operates in.

Figure 7.2. Passerini's Graphic Depiction of GBS's Priorities.
Source: Filippo Passerini and P&G.

Next, there is operational excellence. This highlights the need for doing things right the first time, and to operate as efficiently as possible.

Last, it is essential that GBS leverage the scale that P&G has. This means that GBS needs to build its capabilities in a way that will be relevant when they are even larger than they are now. It also means leveraging the buying scale that the organization has when it procures products or services from others.

These are important messages, and tying these together with this graphic, which is posted in GBS offices around the world, reemphasizes the need for employees to keep these key ideas in mind every day.

Principles Underlying Passerini's Effective Communication

Some good communications principles underlie what GBS has done under Passerini to disseminate its evolving message since 1999.

Clear and consistent. For an organization as large as GBS, it is critical that the message be clear enough for team members to understand no matter their area of focus, the geographic region in which they operate, their tenure with the organization, or their seniority. Even differences in language are taken into consideration, as the terms used are easily translated into the relevant languages across the globe.

Timely. It is also important that the strategy be communicated in a timely fashion. When Passerini releases a strategy, he does not waste time in having the entire team learn about it and internalize it. The rollout is rapid. He works with his communications team to get materials to all relevant locations as quickly as possible. Passerini facilitates the initial sessions, then group discussions follow to help people internalize new ideas at the first opportunity. Even Passerini has been amazed at how effective this process has been. He said, "On several occasions, I have visited remote locations of our operation in the few days following the release of the strategy, and I can speak with a relatively junior person in Turkey, say, and they not only speak clearly and coherently about the plans, but can also connect the dots between their work and the plans."

Relevantly expressed. The preceding quote also points to the need to consider relevance to those receiving a message. Too many plans are written by the senior-most people in the organization, and all too often they are understood only by their peers. This can happen because more junior staff members may not have a clear understanding of the substance of the plans, or because the wording is less than articulate or not adequately fleshed out. Oftentimes, directions are written in a way that automatically makes it nearly impossible to connect the work of a junior person to the plans themselves. A plan will never be followed if it is not understood, so using plain language and anticipating questions before they are asked are important. Imagine an employee new to your organization; is the plan written in a way that they could understand it on day one? They should be able to.

Taking plenty of questions. Passerini anticipates the questions, but also takes plenty of questions, as he gathers the top two hundred people in Global Business Services every quarter. This is an expansive meeting given the many geographic regions represented, but it is critically important to make sure that these people hear from him at the same time, hear each other's questions, ask questions that build upon the thoughts of others, and develop ideas that are based on this common conversation. At the conclusion of these quarterly meetings, the participants are responsible for talking about the plans at greater length with their teams. So they hold sessions akin to the one that Passerini holds for them.

Each strategic plan entails some change, needless to say, even if it is incremental at times. Realizing that this is the case, Passerini suggests that *embracing change is a strategy*. It is human nature to resist change, but for a company as large and complex as P&G, no change means that the competition will soon be ahead, especially since the number of product segments and geographies that the company competes in are so diverse. However, it is critically important that change management be part of the process. This means that wherever changes are articulated, training is put in place where necessary to help people understand and embrace this change. This will only be effective with strong communications discipline behind it. Change as a strategy requires clear and consistent communications about why change is being enacted, how it builds upon the plans of the past, and how it will lead to new value to the company, to customers, and to the shareholders.

The organization is focused on anticipating the changes that are coming and working to always stay one step ahead. "We'd like to always stay on the lookout to see if there is an inflection point coming, and responding to it by asking 'What can we do?' and 'How can we stay in control?'" Passerini explained.

Last, the strategy needs to *place some bets on technology*. IT is a big component of Global Business Services, and Passerini understands that if his organization does not identify the important new technologies that the company needs to embrace in order to bring new value to the business, no one will. "The pace of technology change is increasing, and we need to always keep an eye on the future and a finger on the pulse of this change," said Passerini. He challenges his team and himself to identify which technologies to invest in anew for each plan, on the basis of which technologies can best address the changing needs of the business. This is part of the general push the company has made toward being an innovation factory. Resting too long on the accomplishments of prior years is a recipe for decay. One can argue that technology is the most dynamically changing part of the organization, especially now that consumer technologies have become so influential in the corporate setting, which was the typical path of technology innovation for so many years.

Developing a strategic plan is all well and good, but the development of the plan is the tip of the iceberg. No value is created by putting pen to paper or by putting fingers to keyboard. Strategic plans are supposed to set wheels in motion and to get employees to act, and in many cases act differently. The steps that Passerini drives in his communications of strategy are universally applicable and ensure that plans become actions. The value of pursuing the new technologies, which in many cases may be cutting edge and may entail some risk, must be defined and communicated. IT must also communicate the tie between the new solutions and the priorities of the company as a whole. Connecting these dots is essential to mobilizing the workforce in a united direction. Passerini's communications methods have been world class, from the team he has put together responsible for communications, to the process of spreading the message, to the validation of the resonance of that message, to measuring the value achieved by the plan.

Intel IT's Annual Performance Report

In Chapter Five, I described the outset of Kim Stevenson's tenure at Intel.

Stevenson's ambition for IT to become an equal driver of value to the rest of the organization surpassed the expectations that her peers and superiors had of the department. Given this drive, it may not be surprising that she drew some creative best practices from the corporation at large in order to convey IT strategy.

Stevenson has created the *Intel IT Business Review*, which includes an annual performance report. Comparable to the annual report that is generated for the company as a whole, she describes the year that has passed, the successes that her team enabled, the improvement areas that were uncovered, new sources of innovation, and security updates to be mindful of, to name just a few of the updates.

The first section of the *IT Annual Performance Report* is titled "A Look at the Year Ahead." In it, Stevenson provides slides and a podcast in which the priorities for the year ahead are explained in clear terms. Another section further into this performance report is titled "Intel IT Mid-Year Report," which looks at the year prior. This provides continuity between plans, and allows readers to see what Stevenson had declared to be strategic six months prior and gauge how she and the team did. This level of transparency breeds great confidence in a CIO and his or her team, and it pushes the rest of the organization to be as open and candid.

The report has many other well-thought-out sections. "Intel's IT Environment" is a section with a series of slides providing what is referred to as "a look inside" the operational requirements and needs of the IT department.

Chris Sellers, general manager of Intel IT Information Security, features in a section on security. In a recent version of the report, he discussed Intel's "'protect to enable' security strategy, based on the implicit assumption that compromise is inevitable."

Another section is on the theme of embracing change. In it, David Aires, general manager of IT Operations, explains how Intel IT is embracing the consumerization of IT, and in doing so, becoming more relevant, more influential, and more impactful.

Other sections of the report include

- Design innovation
- User-centered IT
- Possibility thinking
- Intel's supply chain

The recent version also had a special section on big data, with articles, videos, and podcasts covering topics such as

- Intel's big data journey (so far)
- Big data analytics
- Intel IT labs and big data
- Advanced predictive analytics
- One big data strategy
- Self-service business intelligence

You can see that Stevenson has adopted the concept of IT as advisor to the rest of the company. She and her team have taken a critically important topic, and rather than waiting for other business functions to declare what constitutes an opportunity or a source of innovation, IT has put a stake in the ground and provided content that engages the rest of the organization in a compelling and new way. This is a conversation starter, and it draws people toward IT rather than away from it. It leads others to want to engage IT when contemplating these big topics, in this case big data, rather than pursuing these ideas on their own.

Within Intel, the *IT Business Review* and the *IT Annual Performance Report* have been definitive successes. The *IT Annual*

Performance Report is also disseminated among external partners. In a recent version of this report, Stevenson explained,

> I encourage the people in my organization to be "bold" in their thinking and ideas. And when they step up and act bold, they often delight me and our Intel business partners. Recently, a small team took a bold idea and reimagined how we deliver information to our peers and the industry. Historically, we have provided the Intel *IT Annual Performance Report*, a comprehensive report of data and proof points on IT value, provided on an annual, year-in-review perspective. This team asked, 'What would happen if we took a new approach to communicating with our IT industry peers? Could we connect with them more often through social channels and share our best practices as we go instead of the end of the year? Could we build in social sharing and engage with them on their favorite devices?'
>
> The results of their effort—our new Intel *IT Business Review* mobile app (for smart phones) and a digital magazine (for tablets). Going forward, the Intel IT team will engage with you at key points along our journey, sharing insights and best practices and connect you regularly with our IT experts, customers and fellow travelers.[3]

IT cannot succeed alone, and external partners are increasingly a key determinant of whether an IT department will consistently succeed or not. As I have mentioned elsewhere in this book, keeping them in the dark on strategic imperatives means that they will not be able to bring their best ideas that align to your critical imperatives to light in the shortest amount of time possible. The degree of openness that Stevenson suggests is rare, but she and her team have garnered tremendous benefits from it.

This is a practice that more CIOs need to undertake. Equal parts transparency, accountability, and interesting insight—this is a set of processes that you should implement right away!

Leverage Communication Vehicles

Various tried-and-true communications methods are important to leverage as a means of explaining and reiterating IT strategy. Figure 7.3 summarizes some of the main ones.

Vehicle	Within IT or Outward?	Comments	Suggested Frequency or Use
IT Newsletter	Outward	Articles should address important ongoing initiatives as well as status updates from different areas of IT (for example, different divisions or groups, or specific functions such as security).	Monthly
IT Leadership Meeting	Inward	The CIO should meet with other IT leaders on a regular basis. These meetings should be used to not only develop common standards and address common needs, but also address issues from their respective parts of the organization.	Weekly
All-Hands IT Meetings	Inward	Use all-hands meetings to address the overall state of IT (usually on a semiannual or quarterly basis).	Quarterly

Figure 7.3. An Overview of Vehicles.

Vehicle	Within IT or Outward?	Comments	Suggested Frequency or Use
Social Media and Collaboration Technologies	Inward and Outward	Implement social media tools that connect all IT employees across the organization, as well as drawing insights from customers. Use of social media tools can also facilitate the formation of communities of interest and inquiry.	Ongoing
Enterprise IT Knowledge Base	Inward	Establish an enterprise-wide IT knowledge base, and dedicate resources to maintaining it once created.	Update consistently
IT Peer Groups	Inward	Create peer groups for different IT roles to increase collaboration, idea generation, and problem solving.	Ongoing
Project Review	Inward	Hold a review of the project portfolio on a consistent basis that is open to all of IT.	Monthly
Mentoring Program	Inward and Outward	Implement a formal mentoring program across IT and into other parts of the organization to develop personal relationships.	
Blogs	Outward	Use leadership blogs as a means of better establishing web presence and to offer the voice of IT leadership.	Ongoing

Figure 7.3. An Overview of Vehicles. (*Continued*)

Review and Communication Take-Aways

1. Keep plans fresh so that they remain operational:
   - Don't constantly review, but most CIOs don't review plans consistently enough.
   - Small, nimble companies: review often to take advantage of how fast they can change direction.
   - Larger, more established companies: resist complacency.

2. Refine plans on the basis of time and events:
   - Review in the face of outside events such as an economic downturn or regulatory changes and internal events such as acquisitions, divestitures, reorganization, and leadership changes.
   - Communicate perspectives on risk preparedness and innovation, highlighting new technologies to pursue.
   - Reexamine earlier underlying assumptions about the company, economic environment, customers, and so forth.
   - Review extensively at least yearly. Tweak on a regular basis.

3. In reviews, take stock of strategic progress and accomplishments:
   - Ask, "Are strategies working?"
   - Ask, "Has a project achieved its goal and so might be ended?"
   - Ask constituents about their own, IT, and company SWOTs.
   - Communicate your findings.

4. Link time-triggered reviews to budgeting cycles, IT investment council meetings, board meetings, or other relevant gatherings:
   - Try post-project reviews.

5. To communicate strategy, first express it in terms accessible to others throughout the organization.

6. Describe evolving themes in terms of an ongoing story.

7. Note and explain continuities and changes, especially as they might affect tactics present, discontinued, and future.

8. Messages need to be clear, consistent, timely, and expressed in relevant terms.

9. Spread messages through levels of meetings that welcome and respond to lots of questions.

10. Use reliable inward- and outward-directed vehicles with suitable frequency, such as newsletters, meetings, organizational charts, social media and collaboration technologies, enterprise IT knowledge base, mentoring programs, and blogs.

8

The Challenging Work Ahead

I f you have gotten to this part of the book, you may be thinking that what it describes is a lot of hard work. Honestly, it is. What is important to note, however, is that the first iteration is the toughest. Once you've done it the first time you will have established a baseline from which subsequent work will be a process of refinement rather than starting over from scratch. That may be small comfort if you have not yet embarked on the journey. That said, I must ask, What is the cost of not doing this? Is yours a high-growth organization? The price of not having better plans against which to plot your portfolio of investment will be greater in the future than it is today. It is a difficult undertaking today, but it may well be an untenable one next year as the demand for IT grows and the diversity of that growth makes the challenge ever more complex.

If yours is not a high-growth company but rather a laggard in your industry, or if your company will be focusing mainly on cutting costs for the foreseeable future, even so I would argue that the CIO must be at the center of these conversations. In fact, if part of the path toward cost-cutting is to be automation of manual processes, for instance, then the CIO must make the case for augmented budgets for IT in order to decrease costs for the rest of the organization. What better way to determine where the opportunities lie than to have more clearly articulated plans for the entire organization?

In Bad Times or Good

During the economic malaise that commenced in 2008, more companies looked for more opportunities to do things in a more standard, shared way across departments, to create better process and technology standards, and to reduce the technology and vendor footprint. At that point in time, there tended to be a fair amount of "low-hanging fruit," so to speak, as many companies had not been doing this sort of reconciliation during prior good economic times. For many companies, the best CIOs were at the center of these conversations, thinking about how to automate more, to do more in a standard fashion, and to take greater advantage of economies of scale.

Likewise, as the growth prospects for a number of firms improved a few years later, and different divisions of the company started leveraging data analytics software or social media or mobile technology, the best CIOs put themselves in the center of these conversations, and invited a wide variety of constituents to join the conversations so that a strategy for the entire company could be developed and the number of investments to meet the needs of the many would be relatively few.

However, CIOs should not change their way of operating to reflect the vicissitudes of the business cycles. During good times or bad, IT leaders must constantly collaborate with the leaders across the company to promote growth and to ensure that growth is undertaken in an efficient manner.

Consider the example of Automatic Data Processing's CIO. Mike Capone has long had one foot in information technology and the other in the business. He has a bachelor's degree in computer science, but he also has an MBA. He spent time as a vice president of IT at ADP, but he went on to be a general manager of a global HR and payroll outsourcing business within the company. In July 2008, he became ADP's first-ever global chief information officer.

Capone probably did not realize that he was taking on that role on the cusp of the worst economic downturn of his lifetime, but as he was leading the new function he did what any good CIO who is new to his or her role would do: he had a number of conversations with his peers about their needs. He met with customers to understand where ADP had delighted or disappointed them with technology. All the while, he took notes and made sure that IT had a more active role in the planning process with the rest of the organization, while also being more transparent as to their own plans.

When the economy crashed, Capone, like most CIOs, was asked to cut costs, and many painful steps had to be undertaken. That said, he did not forget the many new opportunities that he had identified through his conversations with colleagues and customers that continued well past his honeymoon period as CIO. In early 2009, when most other CIOs were focused only on efficiencies, Capone identified a small cadre of high performers in the IT department and made innovation their primary focus.

It was during this time that Capone recognized the need for ADP to do more with mobile solutions to meet the growing demand of customers to access their information from any device anywhere. He and this overachieving group that he had assembled developed a highly popular mobile application that delighted customers and was downloaded at a record pace. More important to the company culture, Capone also instilled an awareness that, because it understood the strategic opportunities of the entire company, IT always needed to be a source of innovation and could not take a few years off from developing new, technology-enabled products. In the second half of 2012, Capone added the role of corporate vice president of product development to his CIO title, adding a very business-centric role to his one in IT.

Why You, as CIO?

Not long ago, I spoke with Gary Beach, the publisher emeritus of *CIO* magazine. During his long tenure at the magazine, he would poll a wide array of CIOs annually about, among other things, their status in their own companies. The questions asked how many CIOs saw themselves as "game changers" to the businesses that each was a part of. In the roughly fifteen years that the poll has been undertaken, the number of CIOs answering in the affirmative has never been above 9 percent. I am not surprised that CIOs might have suffered from a lack of confidence in the late 1980s or early 1990s, but during current times when IT is so clearly growing in importance, how could this continue to be the case?

Mike Capone exemplifies the IT executive who expands the value of IT to the point where it is only logical that he take over a key business role. Unfortunately, too many CIOs do not feel it is their place to push the rest of the organization to articulate their plans in a better way. However, as I asked near the outset of the book, who is really better suited? The Marketing department, which has primarily an external view? The HR department, which, like IT, works with literally everyone in the company, but which has primarily an internal focus?

IT has the breadth that a department such as HR has, and increasingly it is becoming an internal and external function, as CIOs and their teams are spending more time with customers. Who better than the CIO to take this on from the perspective of playing offense (finding new opportunities and being more proactive in advising the rest of the organization), but also from the perspective of defense and self-preservation (ensuring that the divisions do not make decisions that will have long-term IT implications, requiring IT's support without involving IT in the process).

To a greater extent, I think that CIOs will be asked to be change agents across many companies because of the increased importance of IT in companies, and the growing number of cases of CIOs who have successfully navigated this path.

Strategy: Still the Name of the Game

It's true that Peter Drucker once said, "Culture eats strategy for breakfast." By this he meant, for instance, that if your strategic plans suggest significant changes of one sort or another, as most strategic plans do, if your culture does not tolerate change, then the intransigence of the culture is likely to trump a beautifully articulated strategy. I agree with this sentiment, but believe that a well-articulated strategy is one of the paths to changing that culture.

The way to be on the leading edge of this change and to truly be like those few game changers in the *CIO* poll is to become more strategic. This requires weaving one's self and one's team more into the strategy-setting process of the rest of the organization, to articulate the many ways in which IT can bring those plans to life, to suggest new strategic possibilities to one's peers who head other divisions, and to artfully and clearly articulate the plans that IT has for itself.

As Filippo Passerini of P&G and Kim Stevenson of Intel both noted in earlier chapters, it is important to reflect on the past and present before articulating a plan for the future. No one wants to be told that their past work was not useful, and that the new plan is going to change all that was wrong. Rather, it is better to explain how the important work of the past has led to the present state, and then offer information about the compelling opportunities to seize and pitfalls to avoid in pursuing plans for the future. A well-crafted narrative is what is likely to get people on board and to push in the same direction toward the destination described in the strategic plan.

Sometimes when I speak with executives about the need for a more thoughtful and formal strategy-setting process, I will receive pushback suggesting that taking the time to document strategy is not so meaningful because it is a constant reflection of a moment in time that starts losing relevance before the ink dries on the paper on which it is printed. It is true that strategic plans are not like wine—they do not get better with age—but that does not mean that an absence of a plan is preferable. On the contrary, it is essential to have a clearly defined strategic plan in place that reflects the journey that everyone must take. Changes will be needed, and this book has spelled out how changes required by time or events can be identified and made.

Get Started

I would like to leave you with some encouraging words. Begin this journey as soon as possible. Though it is a daunting one, it is necessary, and it may well lead to tremendous rewards. The sooner this journey begins, the sooner your organization will build the "muscle memory" to do many of the things this book suggests. As conversations with colleagues and customers increase in frequency, new opportunities will be more easily identified and incorporated into plans. As IT becomes more transparent and accountable through its own well-articulated plans and ongoing updates on progress made against them, other divisions are likely to become more transparent and accountable as well, which will benefit IT, but will also benefit the company as a whole.

Why not pursue this change? Why not let this journey for the company begin with the proactive steps of its CIO? It is time for action. I wish you all the best on your World Class IT Strategy journey!

Notes

Chapter 1

1. Statista, "Global Apple iPhone Sales from 3rd Quarter 2007 to 1st Quarter 2014," http://www.statista.com/statistics/12743/worldwide-apple-iphone-sales-since-3rd-quarter-2007/.
2. Author conversation with Gerry Pennell, February 1, 2013.
3. Author conversation with Vivek Kundra, April 19, 2013.
4. Tod Newcombe, "Vivek Kundra, Federal CIO, Addresses State CIOs," *Government Technology*, April 30, 2009.
5. Hansell Saul, "The Nation's New Chief Information Officer Speaks," *New York Times*, March 5, 2009.
6. Author conversation with Vivek Kundra, April 19, 2013.
7. David Perera, "Kundra Releases Federal Cloud Computing Strategy," *FierceGovernmentIT*, February 13, 2011.
8. J. Nicholas Hoover, "Chief of the Year: Vivek Kundra," *Information Week*, December 19, 2009.
9. Author coversation with Jim Whitehurst, Red Hat, March 1, 2013.
10. Various quotes are from author conversation with Tom Georgens, NetApp, December 4, 2013.
11. Various quotes are from author conversation with Greg Carmichael, July 8, 2013.
12. Peter High, "The Emergence of the CIO-Plus," *Forbes*, November 14, 2012.

13. Peter High, "The Most Talented IT Executives Are Advancing Beyond CIO," *Forbes*, March 25, 2013.

Chapter 2

1. Various quotes are from author conversation with Jo-ann Olsovsky, BNSF Railway, June 7, 2012.
2. Chris Davis, "Managing Through Metrics: The Other Sides of SMART," March 2013, http://www.metisstrategy.com /managing-through-metrics-the-other-sides-of-smart -executive-summary/.

Chapter 3

1. All quotes and information in the preceding section are from Peter High, "Google IT's Mission to Empower Googlers with World Leading Technology," *Forbes*, July 22, 2013.
2. Peter High, "Metis Strategy's Forum on World Class IT," podcast interview with Ken Venner, November 7, 2011.
3. Various quotes and assorted information are from author conversation with Bruce Hoffmeister, Marriott, July 1, 2013.

Chapter 4

1. Michael E. Porter, "How Competitive Forces Shape Strategy," *Harvard Business Review*, March/April 1979.
2. Albert Humphrey, "SWOT Analysis for Management Consulting," *SRI Alumni Association Newsletter*, December 2005.
3. Various quotes and information are from author conversation with Chris Laping, Red Robin, April 30, 2013.

Chapter 5

1. Various quotes are from author conversation with Kim Stevenson, Intel, July 23, 2013.

2. Quotes in this section are from Peter High, "CIO-Plus Series: Interview with P&G Group President of Global Business Services and CIO Filippo Passerini," Forbes.com, March 18, 2013.

3. A. G. Lafley and Roger L. Martin, *Playing to Win: How Strategy Really Works* (Boston: Harvard Business School Press, 2013).

4. Lafley and Martin, *Playing to Win.*

5. Gina Chon and Anupreeta Das, "Ecolab to Acquire Nalco for $5.38 Billion," *Wall Street Journal,* July 20, 2011.

6. Author conversation with Stewart McCutcheon, Ecolab, July 17, 2013.

Chapter 6

1. CIO Council, *A Practical Guide to Federal Enterprise Architecture,* February 2001.

2. Jeanne W. Ross, Peter Weill, and David C. Robertson, *Enterprise Architecture as Strategy: Creating a Foundation for Business Execution* (Boston: Harvard Business Review Press, 2006).

3. The Open Group, *TOGAF 9.1*, Chapter 52, "Architecture Skills Framework" (Zaltbommel, Netherlands: Van Haren, December 2011).

4. Ibid.

5. Ibid.

6. Mike Walker, "A Day in the Life of an Enterprise Architect," Microsoft Developer Network, July 2007.

7. Various quotes and information are from author conversation with Matt Stuempfle, Red Hat, January 3, 2014.

8. Various quotes are from author conversation with Brent Stutz, Cardinal Health, January 22, 2014.

9. Various quotes are from author conversation with Cynthia Stoddard, NetApp, January 2, 2014.

10. Dennis Gaughan, "Introducing the Pace Layered Application Strategy Special Report," Gartner Blog Network, February 3, 2012.

11. Author conversation with Tom Georgens, NetApp, December 4, 2013.

Chapter 7

1. Peter High, "Head of Korn/Ferry's IT Officers Practice Makes the Case for CIOs Moving Beyond." *Forbes*, June 17, 2013.

2. Various quotes are from author conversation with Filippo Passerini, P&G, August 30, 2013.

3. Author interview with Kim Stevenson, Intel, July 23, 2013.

Bibliography

Harvard Business Review. *Aligning Technology with Strategy*. Boston: Harvard Business Review Press, 2011.

Heller, Martha. *The CIO Paradox: Battling the Contradictions of IT Leadership*. Brookline, MA: Bibliomotion, 2013.

Karlgaard, Rich. *The Soft Edge: Where Great Companies Find Lasting Success*. San Francisco: Jossey-Bass, 2014.

Lafley, A. G., and Roger L. Martin. *Playing to Win: How Strategy Really Works*. Boston: Harvard Business Review Press, 2013.

Roberts, Dan, and Brian Watson. *Confessions of a Successful CIO: How the Best CIOs Tackle Their Toughest Business Challenges*. Hoboken, NJ: John Wiley & Sons, 2014.

Topinka, Joseph. *IT Business Partnerships: A Field Guide: Paving the Way for Business and Technology Convergence*. N.a.: CIO Mentor Press, 2014.

Waller, Graham, George Hallenbeck, and Karen Rubenstrunk. *The CIO Edge: Seven Leadership Skills You Need to Drive Results*. Boston: Harvard Business Review Press, 2010.

Acknowledgments

This book is nearly sixteen years in the making, as the methodology described herein was born in the summer of 1998 during the course of a collaboration I undertook with United Airlines CIO Bruce Parker. Bruce was gracious enough to take the ideas of a twenty-four-year-old consultant seriously, and worked with me and my team to help shape some of the key early aspects of the strategic planning methodology. Three of his direct reports at the time, Bob Bongiorno, Nirup Krishnamurthy, and Bonnie Henn-Pritchard, went on to become CIOs and IT executives at major corporations in a variety of industries. I would go on to use this methodology with each of those executives in the years that followed, resulting in new facets, new analyses, and new layers of value. It was the success of the early version of this work that gave me the confidence to start my firm, Metis Strategy, in early 2001.

As an IT strategist, I have had the great fortune to collaborate with many chief information officers from leading companies in the United States and abroad. Since 2005, I have had the luck to tell the stories of these incredibly talented men and women through my first book, *World Class IT*, as well as my podcast series, the *Forum on World Class IT*. I am grateful to all of them for sharing with me their insights, a variety of which are noted in this book.

I am blessed to collaborate with the talented team at Jossey-Bass. I especially want to thank Kathe Sweeney, Emilie Herman,

Rob Brandt, and Jeanenne Ray. I also greatly appreciate the efforts of Alan Venable, who suggested many improvements to the way in which this text was organized.

I have been fortunate to have had a great assortment of colleagues over the years who have helped shape these ideas. One of my earliest comrades was Joe Erlinger, who helped create some of the early versions of some of the templates you'll find herein. Sikander Kiani helped edit a couple of the chapters of this book, and I am grateful for his efforts. I especially want to thank my longtime colleagues Alex Kraus and Chris Davis, each of whom has been instrumental in improving the methodology you will read about, and who have added key points that are noted throughout the book. They also acted as keen editors and supporters throughout this project. I am fortune to have each of them as colleagues and as friends.

Last, I want to thank my family. I cherish the love and support of my wife, Michelle, and our sons, Alex and David. I also want to thank my father and mother, to whom this book is dedicated. We are the products of our environment, and they provided me with a wonderful environment in which to learn and remain curious.

The Author

Peter A. High is the founder and president of Metis Strategy, LLC, a CIO advisory firm founded in 2001. He is an expert in business and information technology strategy, and he has been a trusted advisor to a wide array of business and technology executives ranging across *Fortune* 500 companies in various industries. Peter has developed several strategic methodologies that he and his firm have taught clients to use on their own in order to develop and update strategic plans, choose and manage the right portfolio of projects, and ensure that team performance is on the path to world class levels. The methodology described in this book was the one used to launch Metis Strategy.

In December of 2009, Wiley/Jossey-Bass published Peter's book *World Class IT: Why Businesses Succeed When IT Triumphs*, which was named the third best IT book of 2009 by *CIO Insight* and the number one book to read to "be smarter than your boss," according to *Baseline* magazine, among other accolades. Upon publication in China in late 2010, it climbed into the top fifty business books sold in that market.

Since 2008, Peter has moderated a widely listened-to podcast titled "The Forum on World Class IT," which is available through iTunes on a biweekly basis. He writes the "Technovation" column in *Forbes*, and he is a regular contributor to *CIO Insight*. He has also written for the *Wall Street Journal*, *CIO* magazine, *CIO Digest*,

Information Week, and *On* magazine, and has been interviewed and featured in many other periodicals in the United States, Canada, Australia, and China.

Peter is a judge both for *CIO* magazine's CIO 100 Awards and *ComputerWorld*'s Premier 100 Awards.

Peter has been the keynote speaker at many corporate conferences in the United States, Canada, China, India, England, Ireland, and Australia, and he has lectured at several universities, including Georgetown University's McDonough School of Business, the University of Washington (Seattle) Foster School of Business, the University of Maryland's Smith School of Business, Virginia Commonwealth University's School of Business, Purdue University, and the National Defense University.

Peter graduated from the University of Pennsylvania with degrees in economics and history. He lives in Chevy Chase, Maryland, with his wife and their two sons. To try a software product that automates the process described in this book, contact Peter at peter.high@metisstrategy.com.

Index

Page references followed by *fig* indicate an illustrated figure; followed by *t* indicate a table.